MY THREE YEARS IN MANIPUR

MY THREE YEARS IN MANIPUR

Ethel St. Clair Grimwood

GYAN

MY THREE YEARS IN MANIPUR

Ethel St. Clair Grimwood

ISBN : 9788121201353

First Published 1891, reprint 2016 in India by

GYAN PUBLISHING HOUSE

COLLECTION

OF

BRITISH AUTHORS

TAUCHNITZ EDITION.

VOL. 2796.

MY THREE YEARS IN MANIPUR.

BY

ETHEL ST. CLAIR GRIMWOOD.

IN ONE VOLUME.

mountain guns; Cox of ours. Total now, eight British officers; all very nice and jolly; but to our disgust we have to halt here for rest of ours, rest of Ghoorkas, two more guns, and General Graham.

"Cox brought me telegrams of congratulations from Sir Frederick Roberts, General Stewart, commanding Burmah, and Chief Commissioner, saying everything kind and nice they could. I sent in my despatches next day, and so the first act of the Manipur campaign closes.

"My men have behaved splendidly, both in attack, siege, and retreat, and I have recommended all for the Order of Merit. My luck all through has been most marvellous; everything turned up all right, and there was hardly a hitch anywhere. Poor Clinker! He was 300 yards from eight hundred rifles for twenty minutes and never touched, and a shot killed him at full gallop. Now 'bus' (enough) about myself in the longest letter I have ever written."

"Manipur Fort, *April* 28.

"We arrived here yesterday, and found it empty. We gave them such an awful slating on the 25th that they resisted no more either at my place, Thobal, or here. On the 25th I went out from Palel with fifty my men, Sikhs, fifty our Mounted Infantry under Cox, and fifty 2nd-4th Ghoorkas, the whole under Drury, of 2nd-4th Ghoorkas. We had orders only to reconnoitre enemy's position, not to attack, as remainder were to arrive that morning.

"The road ran along the plain due north towards Manipur, with open plain on left and hills right. Saw the enemy on the hills and in a strong mud fort 1,000 yards from hills in the open. I worked along the hills and drove the enemy out of them, as we found them unexpectedly, and had to fight in spite of orders. Then Drury sent on to the general to say we had them in trap, and would he come out with guns and more men and slate them. Then he sent the Mounted Infantry to the left to the north-west of the enemy, and we worked behind the hills to the north-east, thus cutting them off from Manipur. We went behind a hill and waited.

"At 11.30 we saw from the top of our hill

the column from Palel, two mountain guns, and one hundred 2nd-4th Ghoorkas. The guns went to a hill 1,000 yards to the east of the enemy's fort, and we watched the fun. The first shell went plump into the fort; soon they started shrapnel and made lovely practice, the enemy replying with two small guns and rifles. Then we got impatient and advanced, and worked round to their west flank. The guns went on sending common shell and shrapnel into the fort till we masked their fire. The Ghoorkas, also under Carnegy, advanced from south from Palel. We did not fire a shot till within 100 yards, fearful of hitting own men. Then our party charged, but were brought up by a deep ditch under their walls; down and up we scrambled, and when a lot of our men had collected within ten paces of their walls, firing at every head that showed, the enemy put up a white flag, and I at once stopped the fire. Then they sprang up and fired at us. I felt a tremendous blow on the neck, and staggered and fell, luckily on the edge of the ditch, rather under cover; but feeling the wound with my finger, and being able to speak, and feeling no violent flow of blood, I discovered

I wasn't dead just yet. So I reloaded my revolver and got up.

"Meanwhile my Sikhs were swarming over the wall. I ran in, and found the enemy bolting at last from the east, and running away towards Manipur. My men were in first, well ahead of both parties of Ghoorkas.

"After I had seen all the Manipuris near the fort polished off, I sent for a dresser and lay down in one of the huts in the fort. Soon had my clothes off, and found the bullet had gone through the root of my neck, just above the shoulder, and carried some of the cloth of my collar and shirt right through the wound, leaving it quite clean. I was soon bound up, and men shampooed me and kept away cramp. It was only a very violent shock, and I felt much better in the evening.

"As soon as the enemy got clear of the fort the shrapnel from the hills opened fire on them, and when they got beyond, then Cox cut in with his mounted infantry, and only five or six escaped; but poor Cox got badly shot by one of them through the shoulder, but is doing well.

"Carnegy and Grant, of the 2nd-4th, found twenty or thirty of the enemy in a deep hole in the corner of the fort, where they had escaped our men, and in settling them Carnegy got shot through the thigh, and Drury got his hand broke by the butt of a gun. Two of my men were wounded, and two of the 2nd-4th killed, and five or six wounded, I think because they were in much closer order than my men, who were at ten paces interval.

"We gathered seventy-five bodies in the fort and fifty-six near it, and the shrapnel and mounted infantry killed over one hundred. The Manipuris here say we killed over four hundred. So we paid off part of our score against their treachery. We spent the night there.

"They were tremendously astonished and disgusted when they heard in Palel we had had such a fight. The fact is we left them no bolt-hole, and they thought, after their treacherous murder of the five Englishmen at Manipur, that we would give them no quarter, and so every man fought till he was killed.

"Next morning we advanced to my fort at Thobal, and found it deserted; and the royal family and army fled from Manipur as soon as they heard of the action of the 25th. So yesterday, the 27th, we marched in here, my Thobal party, by order of the general, being the first to enter the palace on our side, the Cachar and the Kohima columns arriving from the west and north just before them.

"I, alas! in my dholi, did not get up till two hours after, as it poured all the march, and the mud was awful; but I slept A1 last night, and to-day am feeling fit and well.

"General Collett, commanding the army, came to-day to see me, and said all sorts of nice things to me, and his A.-G. asked me when I would be a captain, and said I would not be one long, meaning I would get a brevet majority. But all these people are very excited now, and talk of my getting brevet rank, and V.C. and D.S.O.; but when all is settled, if I get anything at all I will be content, and it will be about as much as I deserve. I have asked leave if I might stick to my men, as they had stuck so well to me at Thobal. I have had such luck, the men in this regiment will do anything for me, and I hate the idea of changing regiments again, so I may remain if a vacancy occurs.

"I went out for a 'walk' in my dholi this evening, and went round the palace—a very poor place."

CHAPTER XX.

LITTLE remains now to be added to the record of my three years in Manipur, and escape from the Mutiny. Mr. Grant is now a major and a V.C, and never were honours more bravely won. England has given me unstinted praise, and her Majesty has honoured me of her own accord with the Red Cross, of which I am proud to be the possessor.

Shortly after my arrival in England in June, I was invited to Windsor and had an audience of her Majesty, during which I related some of my experiences, which, I believe, interested her. The Red Cross is an honour doubly valuable as having been presented to me by her Majesty in person; but the warm interest she has since been pleased to take in me I look upon as an equally great honour, and my visit to the Queen at Windsor will for ever be remembered as a red-letter day in my existence.

Before I had been many days in England, the Princess of Wales was also kind enough to express a wish to see me, and her royal highness has honoured me greatly by interesting herself in me in many ways; so that though I have lost much, I have received great sympathy; and I know that there are few hearts in England who have not felt for me in my trouble.

But sometimes the thought of the future, and the fate in store for me, seems very dark and dreary. Few of us are without ambitions, and I had mine in the days that are gone; but when they have all been destroyed at one blow, it is difficult to raise up new ones to take the place of the old—difficult to battle for one's self in this eager, hurrying world, when one has grown accustomed to having someone always ready and willing to battle for one; and difficult to accustom myself to a lonely, solitary existence, after four years of close companionship with one whose sole wish was to make my life happy.

Ah, well! life, after all, does not last for ever, and maybe some day we shall awake to find ourselves in a different sphere, where our lost ambitions may be realized, and where disappointment and death have no part.

In this book I have endeavoured to avoid writing anything which may be construed into an accusation or insinuation against any of the persons concerned, whether they be alive or dead. Far be it from me to speak of blame, or to attempt to place any extra responsibility on any one person. It is not in my power to do so, and if it were, I should hesitate.

We know that those five brave men sacrificed their lives sooner than listen to the terms of ignominy and disgrace proposed by their victorious enemies. The touching answer given when the ungenerous proposal was made to them shows that they never wavered from their duty. "We cannot lay down our arms," they said, "for they belong to Government." And each one met his death bravely for the honour of England.

* * * * *

I have since heard of the escape of most of our servants. They were made prisoners and kept by the Jubraj in gaol for some time, but released before the arrival of the troops. Mr. Melville's sad fate filled all with horror, and seemed doubly hard as he had never had anything to do with Manipur before this year, 1891, but merely happened to be in the place at the time.

A new Rajah has been appointed now on an entirely different footing. He is only a little fellow of five years old, a descendant of some former monarch, and it will be many years yet before he can govern the country and the people, and restore the old feelings of peace which existed between our Government and Manipur.

Those by whose orders Mr. Quinton and his companions were murdered have paid the penalty by forfeiting, some their lives, and others their liberty, and order is once more restored.

But in more than one home in England there is sorrow for those who are not. Their vacant places can never be filled up, even though in time, when the grass has grown green above them, we shall learn to think of them not as dead, but as living elsewhere purer, truer, freer lives, unhampered by the sorrows and cares of this world.

Time may, perhaps, do that for us, but meanwhile hearts will ache, and longings will arise for "the touch of a vanished hand, and the sound of a voice that is still," and the hard lesson will have to be learned that nothing is our own—no, not even those who seem part of our very lives, around whom all our tenderest interests and highest hopes cling.

Well for us if, in learning the lesson, we keep our faith and trust in the Being for whose pleasure we were created, and whose right it is to demand from us what we value most. And if, when our time comes, and we look back across the vista of years at all the disappointments and all the sorrows, which, after all, outweigh the happiness in our lives, and can say, "It was all for the best," then the lesson will not have been learnt in vain, and it will indeed be well with us.

THE END.

MY THREE YEARS IN MANIPUR

AND

ESCAPE FROM THE RECENT MUTINY

BY

ETHEL ST. CLAIR GRIMWOOD.

COPYRIGHT EDITION.

WITH PORTRAIT OF THE AUTHORESS.

LEIPZIG
BERNHARD TAUCHNITZ,
1891.

CONTENTS.

CHAPTER XV.

CHAPTER XVI.

CHAPTER XVII.

CHAPTER XVIII.

THREE YEARS IN MANIPUR.

CHAPTER I.

MANIPUR! How well I remember the first time I ever heard the name—a name, too, which was comparatively unknown three short years ago, owing to the fact that it belongs to a remote little tract of country buried amongst hills and difficult of access, far away from civilized India, and out of the beaten track. This is not a geographical treatise, and therefore there is no necessity to dwell much on the exact whereabouts of a place which has already been described more than once. I will therefore attempt no lengthy description, simply stating that the valley of Manipur lies between Cachar, the Kubo Valley, and Kohima, and is surrounded by six ranges of hills which separate it from the tracts of country named. A pretty place, more beautiful than many of the show-places of the world; beautiful in its habitable parts, but more beautiful in those tracts covered with forest jungle where the foot of man seldom treads, and the stillness of which is only broken by the weird cry of the hooluck* or the scream of a night-bird hunting its prey.

We had not been in India many months when my husband was offered the post of political agent at Manipur. We were at the time in a very junior position in Sylhet, a place which had not fascinated either of us in our short stay there; but as a junior officer my husband could not complain. When, therefore, we got a letter one morning offering him Manipur, we were much elated. Visions of the glories heard of, but not seen, floated in front of both our minds. I pictured to myself the dignity of being the mistress of a Residency, of possessing servants in scarlet and gold, with "V.R." on their buttons, and a guard-of-honour to walk out with me whenever I chose. I saw visions of a large house and extensive grounds, and I pictured the ensign of Old

* The hooluck is a black monkey, peculiar to Assam.

England dominating over all. Frank, likewise, had dreams of polo ponies that played of their own accord every day of the week, and visions of many tigers only waiting to be shot, and snipe roosting in the veranda!

Perhaps some may wonder why such dreams should be ours, and why we built such castles in the air. Once, many years before this time of which I write, my husband had passed through Manipur on his way to England. He had spent a couple of days there, and had seen the lake in the compound covered with wild-duck, which were almost as tame as the familiar bird associated, as a rule, in our minds with green peas and the spring. He had played a never-to-be-forgotten game of polo with three royal princes on a ground worthy of Hurlingham, and he had taken it out of the snipe one morning. Small wonder that those two days remained in his memory, and made him long for more like them, when it was his fate to be stationed in an uncongenial spot, where polo comes like Christmas once a year, and which even the snipe desert. And small wonder, too, was it that when the letter came, offering him the coveted post, he jumped at it. How glad we were, and how we hastened to pack up our belongings and depart to the land of so much promise!

Nothing bothered us, not even when our kitchen was blown down bodily in a gale of wind one night, and our new cooking-pans were damaged, and, worst of all, our highly-valued and excellent cook gave notice to quit immediately. The latter though, I am glad to say, reconsidered his decision, and on my promising him extra pay and new cooking-pots, he kindly condescended to link his fortunes with ours for a further period. All's well that ends well, and the extreme sunniness of my temper on that occasion merited a little reward. A flying visit to Shillong, the hill station of Assam and headquarters of the Government of that province, and a hasty return to Sylhet to bid good-bye to the few Europeans there and to collect our possessions, occupied our time until the day arrived which was to see us start on our long journey.

Here in England we consider a journey long that lasts perhaps a day and a half, or even one whole day; but to anyone who has ever been in the remote parts of India, and more especially of Assam, a two days' journey would count as very little. Our journey to Manipur took sixteen days, and hard travelling into the bargain. Up every morning and in our saddles soon after six, with a fifteen-mile ride before us—hail, rain, or sunshine. People in England cannot realize what real hard travelling means. The whole of your baggage in Assam is carried by coolies. They are wonderfully strong, and can take very heavy loads—when they please, that is to say. But a disagreeable coolie can be very disagreeable indeed. We encountered many such, and the first day on our travels it happened that we had more than one unruly specimen.

We started in boats late one night after dinner, and slept on the river, while the boatmen rowed us up stream to a place some twenty miles away, where our horses were to meet us. It sounds rather pleasant travelling by boat at night on a broad smooth river, with the moon shining overhead as only an Indian moon can shine. But the situation loses much of its romance when you know the style of boat that we travelled in.

They are small, awkwardly-built machines, rather of the Noah's-ark type, with a roofing made of bamboo coarsely woven into matting, and so low that it necessitated crawling in on all fours when you wished to retire for the night. Any idea of standing upright had to be abandoned. Once in, you had to lie down and shuffle off your clothes, and tumble into your blankets, which were spread upon the floor. Every time there was any steering to do, the vibration caused by the movement of the rudder awoke you from your slumbers; and, worst of all, the insects that swarmed in the woodwork were most numerous and officious in their unceasing attentions to the unhappy occupants of the boat.

Two of our crew had the misfortune to disagree upon some trivial matter during the night, and as the space for settling their differences was limited to about four square feet on the prow of the boat, the stronger mariner ejected his weaker comrade into the river with much noise, wordy and otherwise. Having ascertained the cause of the squabble, and insisted on the immediate rescue of the fallen adversary from an untimely end, we were allowed to sleep as peacefully as we could until daylight, when we arrived rather cold and very hungry at our first halting-stage, where chota hazri (early breakfast) and our horses awaited us. Then began a struggle between our domestics and the shivering crowd of coolies collected for the purpose of carrying our luggage. With one voice they exclaimed that the Mem-sahib's boxes were quite too enormous to be carried at all—in fact, that there never had been boxes like them before or since, and that we must pay for at least three coolies for every box. My husband made a few observations to them in a somewhat peremptory form, and the end of the matter was that two men were told off for each trunk, and eventually, with many heart-rending groans, our luggage moved off. Now, there is one point which I must touch upon before going on, and it is a point which must strike anyone who has ever travelled in India, and that is the extraordinary habit your rattletraps have of looking disreputable as soon as they come to be mounted on the back of a coolie. Whether it is that the undeniable presence of a large and unsightly bundle of bedding has a demoralizing effect upon the whole, which is not lessened by the accompanying basket of fowls and ducks destined to be your breakfasts and dinners until you arrive at your destination, I cannot say. But be your trunks the most respectable, neat, orderly trunks on the face of this earth, they will look plebeian when they come to be carried on the back of a half-clothed native, and you would scarcely recognise them were it not that your own name betrays you, painted in large white letters on them all, and your horses fail to shy at them in consequence, if they are gifted with ordinary intelligence.

We started off about two hours after our things had left, but we had not gone far when I saw a familiar object lying on the side of the road in the shape of my largest bonnet-box. Further on we spied nearly all our luggage, with the wretched cook doing "sentry go" over it. On inquiring, we found that all our coolies had run away—no one knew where, and it was quite impossible to get them again. Eventually we raised a few more from a police Thana, and had to drive them in front of us the whole way to prevent them bolting too. Consequently we were many hours getting to our destination, and did not get dinner till about nine at night. With few exceptions, our march continued like this every day until we arrived at Cachar, a small station on the Manipur frontier.

CHAPTER II.

CACHAR, or rather Silchar, deserves a description, as it has been of such importance during the recent troubles at Manipur. The town is about one hundred and thirty miles from the Manipur capital, but only twenty-four miles from the boundary. The state of Manipur is separated from the Cachar district by a river called the Jhiri, where we have outposts garrisoned by troops. Silchar itself is not a very large station, though it boasts of more Europeans than most Assam districts, there being a regiment always quartered there besides the usual civil authorities. The district has a very large planting community, and abounds in tea-gardens; and as the planters are constantly in and out, there is a very fair amount of gaiety, especially in the winter months, when there are always two or three race meets, each lasting for a week, which bring people in from far and near.

Silchar has seen much trouble during the last year. In September, 1890, the Lushai disaster occupied everyone's attention, and troops poured through the place on their way to the hills about Fort Aïjal to avenge the treachery of the tribes inhabiting those regions — treachery which resulted in the loss of two valuable lives. A few weeks later curiosity was rife to see the ex-Maharajah of Manipur, who had been driven from his throne by his brother the Senaputti, and was passing through on his self-imposed pilgrimage to the sacred city of Brindhaban on the Ganges, accompanied by three of his brothers. Christmas brought the usual round of races, dances, and dinners with it; but the sound of the Christmas bells had scarcely ceased when the New Year brought tidings of a disaster which caused men's faces to pale, and almost out-rivalled the horrors of the mutiny. But I am anticipating events, and must return to ourselves and our experiences three years earlier.

We stayed two or three days in Silchar on our first arrival there and made some new friends, and were fêted, as is the custom when new-comers arrive at a station in India. Hospitality is a law, and you have only to be English to be assured of a welcome from your fellow-countrymen, who are ready to put themselves, their houses, and possessions all at your service. There are disadvantages, maybe, to be met with in India which are many and great, and one loses much by having to live out there; but one never meets with such true-hearted kindness anywhere else as in India. The narrow prejudices and questioning doubts as to who you are, and what your station in life is, which assail you at home, vanish entirely when you need hospitality out there. The civil list or the army list will tell your position and income, and for the rest you are English, you come from the old country, and all are glad to see you and be kind to you. I am happy to think of the good friends made when I was out there too—friends who were ready to share their pleasures with me, and who were still more ready to help me when the dark days of trouble came and human sympathy was so needed. Their names will ever live in my heart, and may all good luck be theirs!

Our short stay in Silchar came to an end very soon, and we were on our way to Manipur in real earnest by the end of the third day. The first two marches out to the Jhiri were uneventful, and we then found ourselves on the banks of the river, with a vast expanse of forest jungle before us to be traversed the following day. Unluckily, it rained all that night, and when the morning arrived it was still damp and drizzling. We changed our coolies here, and got Nagas (hillmen) to carry the baggage. They were fine-looking men, belonging to the various hill tribes about Manipur. There were Kukis, Tongkhuls, and Kupoës, and they seemed to my uninitiated eyes very alarming people indeed. They wore very few clothes, and their necks were adorned with many necklaces made of gaudily-coloured glass beads. Their ears were split to a hideous extent, and in the loops thus formed they stuffed all kinds of things—rolls of paper (of which they are particularly fond), and rings of bamboo, which stretched them out and made them look enormous.

Their hair was cut in different ways. The Tongkhuls' heads were shaved with the exception of a ridge along the top, which extended to the nape of the neck, and gave them the appearance of cockatoos.

The Kukis' hair was long, and gathered up into a loose and very untidy knot at the back of their heads, and the Kupoës had theirs cut so that it stuck out all round their heads and made them look as though they had fur hats on. *They* made no fuss over the Memsahib's trunks, and I was much amused at the way they all rushed for the bath, which had a flat cover to it, and was easy to carry and cool against their backs. It was a muggy kind of day in the middle of April —a day that invariably brings out legions of horse-flies and gnats and things of that species to worry you and your horses. Worry us they most certainly did. They collected in rows under the brims of our hats and stung our faces, and they settled in swarms on our horses, and what with the dreadful state of the so-called road, and the heat and the flies, we were dreadfully tormented. We had a guard of Manipuri Sepoys with us, who marched along in front of us and helped to lead our horses through the sea of deep mud which covered the road. For seven miles we plodded on like this, and then we came to the first range of high hills and got out of the mud. These hills are the backbone of Assam, and the Manipur ranges are a continuation of those known as the Naga Hills. The highest range on the road to Manipur is about 6,000 feet, but they are all steep, and the road over them is very rough, making riding difficult in places. They are covered with bamboo jungle, and here and there you come across villages, but they are not numerous.

At every five miles the Manipuris had Thanas for the purpose of keeping a look-out against enemies, and acting as stages for the dak-runners. These Thanas were not always fortified, but the larger ones were, and they had been attacked more than once by Lushais out on a head-hunting expedition. There was great excitement at our advent at all the Thanas, and the Sepoys on guard at each stage turned out in style and gave us the "General's salute." They had a particular fondness for bugling, and they exercised it on every possible occasion; but I'm afraid they were not struck with our appearance that day, as we were very tired and hungry, and covered with mud.

We did not get to the end of our march till late in the evening, and we then found we had to cross a river, as our camping-place was on the left bank, and our horses had to be left on the other side. We crossed by means of a bamboo suspension-bridge—a most alarming-looking erection. These bridges are really curiosities. They are made of wire twisted into thick ropes, and stretched from trees on either side of the river at different heights. Bamboos are hung on to the wires close together to form a kind of railing on each side, and these are fastened with cane to the floor of the bridge, which is made of bamboo also, woven into a kind of coarse matting, and although they look most flimsy and airy erections, they are really very strong, and can carry any number of men on them at once, and animals too, if necessary. They are a great height from the water, which you can see between the chinks of the matting as you walk across, and they have an unpleasant fashion of swinging violently when you are in the middle of them, making it very difficult to keep your footing. I did not like going over it at all, and tumbled down in the most awkward fashion more than once, much to the amusement of the Manipuris, who laughed very heartily.

It began to rain shortly after we had arrived at the rest house, a large barn-like place built of bamboo also, with one doorway and no windows of any kind, and a mud floor. Not an atom of furniture graced this abode, and there was nothing to be done but to sit down on the ground and wait until our luggage should arrive—very hungry, and generally out of sorts. Nothing came in until nine at night, when the cook arrived with the kitchen paraphernalia, and we had a sort of dinner on the floor, and then had to wait until two in the morning for our heavy baggage and beds, which were travelling on elephants. It was a dreadful four hours, for in the meanwhile swarms of mosquitoes and sandflies came out and attacked us—hands, faces, and, in fact, any part of us that was not covered. The delay was caused by the road being too steep and slippery for the elephants, and their having to be unloaded five or six times—a most tedious operation.

About three in the morning we got our beds put up and turned in, longing for sleep, but I hadn't been there an hour before the rain, which had poured down in torrents ever since dinner, made its appearance through the roof and descended upon my head. So we had to get up and move everything, and then were able to sleep in peace for the remainder of the night. Of course, all idea of going on the next day was out of the question, as servants, coolies, and elephants were all too tired, and, to add to this, the rain never ceased, so I made the best of things and stayed in bed all day, while the coolies busied themselves in making me a dooly out of bamboos, as we found that my horse had got a sore back from his long climb the day before, and my husband decided that it would be better to have me carried the rest of the way. I had time to notice particularly our escort of Manipuri Sepoys during our halt at this place. We were supposed to have thirty men altogether, but I never saw more than twelve. When marching, they had counted themselves over twice by running on ahead directly they had presented arms once, and going through the same performance round the corner, fondly imagining that we should be under the impression that we had double the number with us. Their uniforms were limited. There were about three complete ones amongst them, and the remainder adorned themselves in confections of their own. When halting, we were provided with a sentry to keep guard over us all day, and he was relieved about every three hours, which gave rise to a most amusing scene. A dirty-looking individual came up to the Sepoy on duty, and saluted him with the ordinary native salaam. The sentry then proceeded to divest himself of his uniform coat, belt, etc., and rifle, which he threw down on the ground; whereupon the dirty-looking person picked them up, hastily put them on his own manly form, and, having done so, came up to where we were sitting and saluted in fine style. The other man had meanwhile disappeared. At night we had two sentries, and they frequently asked us whether they might mount guard in the veranda of our hut. This meant that before very long they would both be fast asleep upon the floor, snoring so loud that we were awakened.

When marching, each man went as he pleased and whatever route he pleased. If he were of a lazy turn of mind he slid down all the short cuts, but we generally had one or two walking in front of us, one of whom invariably possessed a bugle, which he made the most of by giving us selections on it from his own imagination. I believe he meant well. Their rifles were carried over their shoulders, and their worldly possessions were done up in a cloth and slung on to the end of them in large bundles. The Manipuri Sepoy was no doubt a very funny animal indeed.

We left our wet camp at the Makru River the next day, very glad to get out of it, and proceeded on our journey towards Manipur. Every day was the same: up and down hill all day and a bamboo hut at night; but our experiences of the first day had taught us wisdom, and we put the things which we wanted most upon coolies, and the elephants carried the rest, as they went so slowly. The Nagas used to swarm out of their villages as we came along to see us, and they were especially interested in me, as many of them had never seen an English lady before. Seven days in the hills, and the eighth brought us at last to the topmost ridge of the last range, and then I had my first glimpse of the valley of Manipur lying beneath us, looking delightfully calm and peaceful in the afternoon sunshine. It looked so beautiful to us after the hills of the previous seven days, stretching away smooth and even as far as the eye could see, and we stopped on the top of the hill some time for the pleasure of looking at it. We could distinguish far away in the plain the white walls of the Maharajah's palace, and the golden-roofed temple of his favourite god. Just below us stretched the blue waters of the Logtak Lake, studded with islands, each one a small mountain in itself. Villages buried in their own groves of bamboo and plantain-trees dotted the plain, and between each village there were tracts of rice-fields and other cultivation. The whole valley looked rich and well cared for, and we longed for the next day, which was to see us at our journey's end.

We were met at the foot of the hill by ten elephants and a guard of fifty Sepoys, under the command of a high officer of state called Colonel Samoo Singh, who was one of the most hideous old gentlemen I have ever seen. However, he was politeness itself, presenting us with large baskets of fowls and vegetables, and escorting us to the rest-house, to which we all went mounted on elephants gaily rigged out in red cloth. I wanted to go on the same elephant as my husband, but the interpreter said "his Excellency the Colonel Sahib" would not like it if we did not make use of *all* the elephants brought out for our glorification, so I proceeded in solemn dignity behind my husband's quadruped. The old colonel came up to the house with us, as also did the guard of honour; and then after a final salute they all departed and left us to our own devices.

Early next morning we were up and ready for the last seventeen miles into Manipur. We had tried to smarten ourselves up as much as possible, as we were to be met by some of the princes before we reached our journey's end, but, alas! a mischievous rat had busied himself during the night by eating a large hole in my husband's hat and all the fingers off my right-hand glove, and we could not get at our boxes to rummage for others, so we had to go as we were.

The old colonel rode with us, and seven miles from Manipur we were met by four princes. They had had a small hut built, which was nicely matted and arranged with chairs. As we rode up, the four royalties came forward to meet us, amidst much blowing of trumpets and presenting of arms by their several guards of honour. This was my first introduction to the Senaputti of Manipur, and little did we foresee the terrible influence he was destined to bear on our future! He was not a very striking-looking personage. I should think he was about five feet eight inches in height, with a lighter skin than most natives, and rather a pleasing type of countenance. He had nice eyes and a pleasant smile, but his expression was rather spoilt by his front teeth, which were very much broken. We liked what we saw of him on this occasion, and thought him very good-natured-looking. The other brothers did not strike us at all, and there were so many people there, including important officers of state, that I became confused, and ended by shaking hands with a Sepoy, much to that warrior's astonishment.

We were escorted to the reception-barn by the princes. The Senaputti was the only one who could speak Hindostani amongst them, and my husband was able to talk to him, but the others only knew Manipuri, so contented themselves with smiling continuously, and I followed suit by smiling back, and it didn't tire any of us. They presented us with an enormous quantity of things, and I do not know how many baskets of fowls, ducks, and vegetables they didn't give us, for they seemed unending. At last, after more hand-shaking, which entirely ruined my already finger-less glove, some polite speeches from my husband and more amiable smiles from me, we mounted our horses and, accompanied by our four royal friends and their retinue, rode into Manipur. A salute of twelve guns was fired on our arrival, and after we had taken leave of the princes at the entrance to the Palace we turned into the gates of the Residency, and felt that our journey was really at an end.

CHAPTER III.

I ALWAYS think a great deal depends on one's first impressions of anything, be it place or people. One is struck with a house or a garden if it looks pleasant at first sight, even though a closer acquaintance with it may bring disappointment. My first impressions of our house and surroundings on this occasion were of the most favourable description. A long carriage-drive led up from the entrance-gate to the house. There were trees each side, and a delightful stretch of grassland dotted about with deodars and flowering shrubs, with a tennis-court in the centre on the right. A hedge of cluster roses all in blossom divided the outer grounds from the flower-garden surrounding the house, at the end of which was a small lake with an island in the middle of it, where, late as it was, a few wild-duck were still swimming about. We cantered our horses up the drive to the entrance, a long flight of steps covered by a porch, over which grew a beautiful Bougainvillia, whose gorgeous purple blossoms entirely hid the thatch with which the porch was surmounted. The Residency was a long low house with a thatched roof. The walls were painted white, and the wood-work picked out in black. A veranda surrounded it, comfortably matted and strewn about with rugs and skins. In front of the house there was a circular lawn covered with flower-beds blazing with colour, and at the end of the lawn was the flagstaff of my dreams and the ensign of Old England waving proudly in the breeze. To us, fresh from the jungles of the previous nine days, the place seemed beautiful, and even after we had grown accustomed to it, we always returned to it with a fresh sense of pleasure. The inside of the house was equally charming, and after our little hut at Sylhet it seemed a mansion. The red-coated servants were all in attendance, and a couple of Ghoorka orderlies, so that my aspirations in that direction were amply satisfied.

In a very few days we had shaken down most comfortably. We had brought with us everything we possessed, and I soon had as pretty a drawing-room as anyone could wish for. The next thing my husband had to do was to make friends with the Maharajah. For this purpose a durbar was arranged, and it took place about two days after we had been there, at eight in the morning. It was a very imposing function indeed. Red cloth was spread all over the veranda and on the front steps, and our whole escort of sixty Ghoorkas was drawn up on the front lawn. The Maharajah arrived with a grand flourish of trumpets, attended by all his brothers, and accompanied also by a large following of Sepoys, slaves and ministers of state, each of the latter with his own retinue. The Maharajah was a short, fat, ugly little man, with a face something between that of a Burmese and a Chinaman—rather fairer than the Bengal natives, but much scarred with small-pox. He was dressed very simply in white—a white coat with gold buttons, and a very fine white muslin Dhotee.* He had a large white turban on his head, in which was stuck a spray of yellow orchids. Gray woollen stockings covered his legs, fastened at

* Dhotee—the usual dress a native wears instead of trousers.

the knee with blue elastic garters with very fine brass buckles and little bows, and his feet were encased in very large roughly-made laced boots, of which he seemed supremely proud.

His eldest brother, the Jubraj, was a second edition of himself, only stouter and uglier. Next in order rode the Senaputti, whom I have already described, and he was followed by five younger brothers. My husband had to go to the outer gate to meet his highness with his hat off, where he shook hands with all the princes, and then walked with the Maharajah back to the house and into the durbar hall, which was in the centre of the Residency. The whole durbar, being only a complimentary ceremony, did not last more than ten minutes, but before he left the Maharajah expressed a wish to see me; so I appeared and shook hands with them all, and smiled amiably, as I did not know enough of the language then to speak to them. They all stared at me very solemnly, as though I were a curious kind of animal, and shortly afterwards they took their departure.

I shall not attempt a detailed account of our life at Manipur, as it was very monotonous and uneventful. We got to know the princes very well. My husband played polo with them, and I frequently rode with them. The Senaputti in particular was our very good friend. There was something about him that is not generally found in the character of a native. He was manly and generous to a fault, a good friend and a bitter enemy. We liked him because he was much more broad-minded than the rest. If he promised a thing, that thing would be done, and he would take the trouble to see himself that it was done, and not be content with simply giving the order. He was always doing little courteous acts to please us. On one occasion I mentioned to him that I had been very much frightened by a lunatic in the bazaar, who was perfectly harmless, but dreadfully deformed as well as insane. He used to spring out upon you suddenly, making terrible grimaces, which was not pleasant, and he frightened me several times. I noticed after speaking to the Senaputti about him that he had not been in the bazaar for a long time, and afterwards I was told that the Prince had ordered him to be kept at home in the evenings, at the time we usually went out for a walk.

Another time I had been very ill, and when I was getting better, kind inquiries came every day from the Senaputti, accompanied by half a dozen small birds which he thought were eatable, as he had often seen my husband bring snipe home. The birds were useless, of course, but I valued the kind thoughts which prompted him to send them. If anything went amiss with my husband's polo-ponies, the Senaputti was quite ready to send him as many as he wanted of his own, and he always mounted any visitor who might by staying with us and wish for a game. He was a keen sportsman and a capital shot. In the cold weather he often organized a week's deer-shooting for my husband, to which I always went, and very good fun it was. The Senaputti would meet us at the place with a number of elephants, and we used to start very early in the morning, and generally returned with a good bag. Bigger game was scarcely known in the valley. Occasionally a stray tiger would wander down and kill a bullock or two, the news of which was immediately conveyed to the Maharajah and a shooting-party organized. A number of men kept for the purpose would start out to the spot where the tiger was supposed to be with nets and enormous spears. They surrounded the bit of jungle first with nets and afterwards with a strong bamboo fence, which, when erected, enabled them to remove the nets. The whole of the royal family then arrived and ourselves, and ascended into little platforms built up very high off the ground to be safely out of reach of the tiger should he escape; and then, with much blowing of trumpets and shouting, the fun began. The jungle inside the fence was then cut down, each cutter being protected by another man armed with an enormous spear. By degrees all the jungle was cut and the tiger forced to appear, when the occupants of the platforms all shot at him at once and ended his career. Sometimes the tiger was speared by the men inside the fence, but the poor beast always had ten or twelve wounds in him when we came to examine him. It was exciting, but it was not sport, and I always felt sorry for the tiger. Whenever I was present the Maharajah presented me with the skin and claws, and I got quite a collection in my three years at Manipur.

The princes always seemed to like our taking

an interest in their concerns, and they frequently visited us, even sometimes on Sundays with a small following, and without any ceremony. Their people remained in the veranda, and they used to come into the drawing-room and talk to us, and look at our photographs and my husband's guns.

Any new invention in the latter pleased them immensely, and they immediately wished to know where the weapon was made and all particulars. They generally stayed with us some time on these occasions. Two or three days afterwards they would ask my husband to shoot or ride with them, and we always saw something of them during the week. On one occasion I mentioned to them that I had never seen a shell fired, so they got the Maharajah to arrange for a field-day, and we rode out to their own rifle-range, and saw their two mountain-guns brought out with different kinds of shell, and fired by the Senaputti himself.

When I think over the events of the last few months, it seems difficult to realize the friendly terms on which we had ever been with the Court at Manipur. How little we could foresee the terrible destruction those same guns were to bring upon our peaceful home in the near future! I was so delighted that day at watching the effect of a shell on the hill we were firing at, and the Manipuris got the range very well, almost every shot taking effect. We were out that morning four or five hours, and all rode back together. The Maharajah rode a beautiful pony on a gold saddle, with large flaps on each side to protect his legs, also of gold. The pony's bridle was made of gold cord, and his head and back covered with balls of soft white cotton. These saddles are really curiosities, and are peculiar to Manipur. The balls of cotton are arranged to protect the pony's sides from being hit at polo, and the whole turn-out is very well made, though rather heavy for the small steeds. It was a fine sight to see the Senaputti play polo. He was very strong; in fact, the Manipuris used to tell us that he was the strongest man in the country. He could lift very heavy weights and throw long distances, and to see him send the ball skimming half across the ground with one hit was a very pretty sight. He could do strokes that few Manipuris knew, which is saying a great deal, for an average player at Manipur can beat most Englishmen. The Senaputti was a magnificent rider, and he was always mounted on beautiful ponies. He wore a very picturesque dress for polo—a green velvet zouave jacket edged with gold buttons, and a salmon-pink silk Dhotee, with white leather leggings and a pink silk turban. He had long hair, which he used to twist up into a knot at the back of his neck, and he always looked very nice on these occasions. All the princes played polo. There was one called Zillah Singh, a boy of about seventeen, whom we used to call the Poem. He was a slight, graceful-looking lad, and he used to ride a tiny mite of a pony, and never troubled himself with too many garments. His turban was always coming off, and his long black hair streamed in the wind as he flew about all over the ground. Even the little son of the Maharajah used to play. He was a dear little fellow, of about eight years old, and once a week there was generally a youngsters' game, in which all the little royalties used to perform, and remarkably well too, considering how young most of them were. My husband played regularly twice a week, all the year round. The Senaputti liked to play for stakes, which were generally muslin cloths or turbans. These were all hung up at the end of the ground, and when the game was ended, the winning side were presented with them, and the losers had to pay for them, which gave an interest to the game, and made both sides play up.

I have said more about the Senaputti than the other princes, because he was the one of them all that we knew intimately. He could speak Hindostani well, while the other princes spoke nothing but their own language, and when we first went to Manipur my husband, of course, didn't know a word of Manipuri, so had to speak to them through an interpreter. He did not lose much time in setting to work to learn it, and he had an old pundit* who used to come every day to give him lessons. This old gentleman was rather a character. His name was Perundha Singh, and he deprived Government of fifty rupees annually, by virtue of calling himself "Burmese Interpreter to the Political Agent," which designation he had engraved on a brass

* Pundit—tutor or interpreter, who will coach you in a language.

plate which he wore on the front of his belt. Whether he really knew Burmese was another matter, but he had certainly been in Burmah, and had seen some fighting there and even got wounded himself. He never turned up on wet days, because the bullet, which, he affirmed, had never been extracted, got affected by the damp and became rusty, causing him much pain and preventing his sitting down. I had a grand idea of learning Manipuri too, but the old pundit used to pay me such florid compliments over the extreme rapidity with which I was picking up the language, that my husband thought I should learn it before he did, and said we must have our lessons at different times, which I found rather dull work, so ceased them altogether. The old pundit was a grand gossip. He had a thousand stories of the good and evil deeds of all the Sahibs who had been before us, and I must honestly confess the deeds seemed chiefly evil ones. He invariably ended up by saying that there never was, and never would be, such a good and excellent Sahib as the present one, which judicious piece of flattery he hoped would be productive of great pecuniary results.

CHAPTER IV.

SUCH was our life at Manipur. It seldom varied day by day. We used to ride every morning, and directly after breakfast go the round of the place, visit the stables and kitchen-garden, and feed all the animals, from the horses down to the two little otters, which were so tame that they followed us about like dogs. What would life in India be without one's animals, I wonder? We were never tired of collecting around us all kinds of creatures, and the natives got to know it, and used to bring us anything they caught. We had three monkeys, little brown fellows, which were my delight. They lived during the day in boxes nailed to posts, and were tied by ropes long enough to enable them to run up and down. Sometimes they got loose, and we had a long chase to get them again, as we could not leave them to do their pleasure upon our garden. One of them was so clever that we had to get him a chain to fasten him by, as he could undo any knot, and gnaw any rope in half in no time. He used to untie the rope and then look cautiously round, and if he saw anyone watching him he would sit on the end he had undone and pretend to be deep in the mysteries of his toilette; but if no one were looking, he would rush off to a large bed of sunflowers on the front lawn and snatch at the blossoms, tearing them to pieces, and strewing the petals all over the place. After this he would make for the house, and, if he were not discovered, run into whatever door or window happened to be open and do dreadful damage to anything that took his fancy. Directly he was seen there used to be a grand hunt after him, when he would betake himself to a particular tree in the grounds, clamber up to the very top, where the branches were too thin to bear any man, and remain there making the most hideous faces at us below. We had to station a man to watch him, as if everyone disappeared he would immediately come down and do more mischief. Sometimes it would be a whole day before the young ruffian was caught, but he generally came down for his evening meal, and then was captured. All three monkeys slept together on a beam in the roof of my bedroom veranda, and they were as good as any watch-dog, for if anything came into the veranda after dark they would begin chattering and making a great commotion. Poor little monkeys! I cannot bear to think of what their fate must have been.

We had a bear, two otters, a tame deer, and two large gray and red cranes, besides the monkeys. The bear was a small ball of black fluff when he came to us, with tiny teeth that could not hurt. We brought him up on milk and rice, and he grew a huge beast. I was a little afraid of him when he grew up. He was always getting loose, and was almost as difficult to catch as Jacko. When he was caught, it was very amusing to see him standing up behind his post playing hide and seek with the servant who was tying him up. He used to put his paw round the post and give the man's bare leg a friendly pat, which must have been very painful, and he stood all the while upon his hind-legs. He got very fierce as he grew older, and one day I was out in the garden gathering flowers and suddenly noticed the Chupprassies and orderlies flying towards the house—a proceeding that always happened directly the bear was at large. He very soon spied me out, and came rushing towards me, and I began to run; but long before I could get to the house he had overtaken me. I threw the flowers I had collected behind me, hoping that he would stop for them, but he just sniffed at them and then came on. He caught me up in a moment and clawed at my back, and tore my jacket all the way down. Fortunately it was a very cold day, and I had put on a thick winter coat, which saved me from getting badly clawed; but he gave me some nasty scratches. Luckily the Ghoorka orderly saw it from the house, and ran up and beat him off; and then the other servants came and captured him and chained him up. So my husband said we must get rid of him, and the next day he was conveyed away by four Nagas and a couple of Ghoorkas to a hill covered with jungle about fifteen miles away and let loose there, with a heap of rice and a lot of plantains to keep him going.

The next day we heard that the Manipuris had kept a holy festival on the identical hill, but we never asked whether they had seen our poor bear afterwards, and we never heard of him again. Our large grounds were a great delight to us at Manipur. We had quite a park at the back, with fine large trees and bushes of gardenias and roses and oleanders. The kitchen-garden was separated from the rest of the grounds by a wall which ran all round it. It always reminded me of an English garden with fruit-trees growing on the wall, and English vegetables all the year round. We had nine gardeners, or Malis, as they are called in India.

Talking of them reminds me of an amusing incident which happened in connection with them. They were Nagas belonging to one of our villages which lay at the back of the Residency grounds, between us and the river. The Nagas never burden themselves with too many clothes, and these in particular wore little beside a necklace or two. I mentioned this fact to a spinster lady friend of mine on one occasion, and she was so horrified that she sent me shortly afterwards nine pairs of bathing-drawers to be given to them. They were very beautiful garments; some had red and white stripes, and some blue, and they were all very clean. I presented them gravely one morning to my nine Malis, and a few days after I went into the garden in the evening and found two of the men at work. One had made a hole in his bathing apparatus and had put his head through it, while his arms went into the places for the legs, and he was wearing it with great pride as a jacket; and the other had arranged his with an eye for the artistic on his head as a turban. After this I gave up trying to inculcate decency into the mind of the untutored savage. We had a good many Naga servants. My second Khitmutghar* was a Naga, and a very excellent servant he was too, except when he was drunk, which I am sorry to say was very often. If we were going into camp, or if we had just returned, were the particular occasions which, in his mind, were the ones of all others to be celebrated with much spirituous fluid. A message would come from the village to say that Mecandaï (the gentleman in question) was very dangerously ill—in fact, that he was not expected to live through the day. At first my sympathies were all aroused in his cause, but after a little experience I dis-

* Khitmutghar—butler, table-servant.

covered the nature of his illness, and had him conveyed to the house. The native doctor was then sent for, and if he said the man was ill he was put into the hospital, if not, he went under military escort to the quarter-guard.

The Nagas will drink anything, but the stronger it is the better they are pleased. They have a beverage of their own which they make of fermented rice water. They can drink great quantities of it with no bad effect at first, but they get very drunk on it if they go beyond a certain limit. They call this liquor Zu, and I have heard my husband say he found it very refreshing after a long hot march; but I never had the courage to touch it, as they offered it to one out of a bottle that was never cleaned and that everybody drank from. I suppose to a Naga there is nothing more delicious than roast dog washed down with quarts of this Zu. Poor doggies! They are only kept to be eaten. They are well fed while they are growing up, and then, when they are ready to be eaten, they are starved for a day. At the end of this they are given an enormous feed of rice and the remains of a former comrade, perhaps, which they eat up ravenously; and then the head man of the village gives the victim a blow on the head and converts him into curry and rice. On one occasion we were going up to our hill bungalow, and our village Nagas, wishing to do us honour, erected a triumphal arch at the entrance to our garden. Fortunately I looked up at it before going under, and saw, to my horror, the head of a dog, which had just been cut off, hanging in the centre of the erection, whilst his four paws and tail graced the sides, and the whole archway was so low that I should have touched the top of it as I rode under. I dismounted, however, and walked through.

The hill bungalow mentioned was situated about fifteen miles from Manipur. It was about 6,000 feet above sea-level, with a delightfully cool climate all the year round, though the rainfall was excessive during the summer months, and damp mists came up from the valley below, hiding even the garden round the house, and making the place very cold. Still, it was pleasant to be able to get away up there for a few days' change from the heat at Manipur, and we generally went up from Saturday till Tuesday every week. The village below the house belonged to us, and rejoiced in the name of Khan-jhubkhul. We had some five or six villages, which were given us by the Maharajah, the inhabitants of which worked for us. They were situated in different parts of Manipur, and we found it very convenient. The Nagas preferred working for us to working for the Maharajah, as we paid them for their labour, whereas the durbar considered it as revenue, and gave them nothing. At the same time, the way the Manipuris managed all the hill-tribes about them was very creditable. Every village had to work for the Rajah so many months in the year —about four. Some had to cut wood, and bring so many bundles in for the place; others had to give so much rice, or go down to Cachar or to Kohima for trading purposes, and each tribe had its own duties. This system extended throughout Manipur, and not only amongst the hill-tribes, but also among the Manipuris themselves, and was called "Lalup." In return for their services they got their land rent free, and were not restrained from trading in their own interests as soon as they had performed their "Lalup" for the Maharajah. It was a system that answered very well, and the people seemed well-to-do and contented.

The women did all the hard work, as a rule. They wove all their own and their husbands' clothing, and cooked and looked after the house generally, besides working in the fields and coming every evening to the big bazaar* with merchandise for sale or exchange. No men were allowed to sell in this bazaar with the exception of a few Bengalee traders, who sat in a different part of the market and sold cloths. It was a pretty sight in the evening to see all the women hurrying along with their wares on their heads, and their little babies slung on their backs. They sat in long rows in the bazaar, and it was divided up in a most methodical way. Vegetables and fish occupied one end, and cloths and jewellery the other, and the whole of the female population turned out, and even the princesses occasionally sold in the bazaar. The princesses were more numerous than the princes, as each of the latter had several wives. The Senaputti was supposed to be the happy owner of nine wives, and the others had almost as many.

* Bazaar—market.

The eldest daughter of the Maharajah was about fifteen. She very often came to see me, in company with nine or ten other girls of the same age, of whom more than half were royalties. The Senaputti used to bring them, and they loved running all over the house, examining everything. They liked most of all to go into my bedroom and try on my clothes and hats, and brush their hair with my brushes, admiring themselves in my long looking-glass. They used to be very much surprised to find that my dresses would not meet half-way round their waists. The Senaputti generally waited in the drawing-room talking to my husband. After the party had explored my room, we used to rejoin the others, and take them all out into the garden, allowing them to pick the flowers, and decorate each other, and then my husband would photograph them. They were always amused with the monkeys and rabbits, the latter particularly, as those animals are wholly unknown in Manipur. In fact, these Manipuri children were very much like any other children in their delight at seeing new things. They liked going into the dining-room when the table was laid for dinner, and asking us what all the knives and forks and spoons were used for; and they enjoyed sitting on the sofas and in the big armchairs, "just like the Memsahib," they said.

Once we had a water-party on the lake in the grounds. The big pink water-lilies were in full bloom, and we had about five boats crammed with these children and some of the little princes, and we all pelted each other with water-lilies and got very wet, and enjoyed it immensely. Of course it was always a drawback not being able to offer them anything to eat or drink, as their caste forbade them taking anything of the sort; but we used to give them flowers, and Japanese fans, and beads, and those kind of things, with which they were very delighted. Some of the Manipuri girls are very pretty. They have long silky black hair as a rule, and fair complexions, with jolly brown eyes. They cut their hair in front in a straight fringe all round their foreheads, while the back part hangs loose, and it gives them a pretty, childish look. They dress very picturesquely in bright-coloured striped petticoats fastened under their arms, and reaching to their ankles. Over this a small green velvet zouave jacket is worn, and when they go out they wear a very fine muslin shawl over their shoulders, and gold necklaces and bracelets by way of ornament. Very pretty these little damsels look as you meet them in twos and threes along the road going to their dancing-lessons, or to market or temple. Every child is taught to dance in Manipur. They cease when they marry, but up till then they take great pride in their nautches.

The Manipuris do not shut up their women, as is the custom in most parts of India, and they are much more enlightened and intelligent in consequence. As soon as a woman marries she puts back her fringe, but no other restrictions are laid upon her. They do not marry until they are fifteen, and I have seen girls of seventeen unmarried. From going so often through the bazaar in the evenings, I got to know several of the women very well and they liked my coming and having a chat to them. I learnt all their little troubles and anxieties — how so-and-so's baby was teething and generally ailing, and how someone else's had grown an inch, or who was going to be married, and who had died. I liked talking to them, and I learnt a good deal of the language by doing so.

CHAPTER V.

From April to the end of October was the rainy season in Manipur, and from October till the end of March the weather was as perfect as could be, very cold, and yet bright and sunshiny, with never a drop of rain to trouble one. All our winter went in camp. We used to go out for a month at a time, and then return to the Residency for a few days before starting out again in another direction. We generally managed two trips to the Logtak Lake. This lake lay to the south of the valley, a day's journey by boat, or two days' if one rode. We preferred the boating. We used to start off early in the morning and ride about fifteen miles, where the boat would wait for us, with all our luggage packed in one end of it, and a well-filled lunch-basket to keep us going by the way. These boats were long and narrow, and were called "dug outs," because each one was hollowed out of a single tree. We spread the bottom with lots of straw, and put rugs and pillows on the top, and then lay down on them and found it very comfortable.

About five in the evening we arrived at the mouth of the river, and had generally to wait some time there to allow the wind, which always got up in the evenings, to subside, as the lake was too rough to cross while it was blowing. Even when we did cross, two hours later, the waves kept breaking into the boat, and we had to set to work to bale the water out. I don't think I shall ever forget the first time I saw the lake. We did not arrive till late, and the moon was high up in the heavens, shedding a glorious silvery light on the broad expanse of waters, and making the islands, each one a small mountain in itself, appear shadowy and far off. Far above our heads flew strings of wild geese going off to feed, and uttering their strange hoarse cry as they flew. Here and there as our boat shot past some sheltered nook or tiny islet two or three ducks would paddle out, scenting danger, and curious water-birds would rise from the swampy ground and noiselessly disappear in the far distance. But the stillness on all around us, and the beautiful lake, whose surface the now dying wind still gently ruffled, had a great effect upon one's imagination, and I was quite sorry when we shot through a narrow creek and came suddenly upon the camp. Our tents were pitched on one of the largest and most beautiful islands, under a big tree, and at the end of a long village, which was built picturesquely on the shore of the lake. The villagers and our servants came down to help us out of our boats with torches and the inevitable bugler, who played us up to our tent in grand style. We were very glad to get in and find an excellent dinner awaiting us, and still more pleased to get to bed. Every day we used to start out at six in the morning, before the mist had cleared—I in one boat, and my husband in another—and creep round the little islands after duck, and we generally returned with a large bag. In two days once my husband got eighty-two ducks and thirty geese. He did great execution with an eight-bore he had, and generally knocked over half a dozen or so at a time with it. Duck-shooting is very exciting, and hunting wounded birds a lengthy operation. They let you come quite close to them, and you think you have got them safely, when they suddenly dive under your boat and appear again yards off; and by the time you have turned your boat and gone after them again they are still farther away. I never liked it when we had caught them and they used to be consigned to my husband's boat, as I could not bear to see them killed. Sometimes they were so tame that we let them alone, as it seemed butchery to shoot them.

One year when we went to the Logtak the Pucca Senna (the Maharajah's third brother) asked if he might come too. We were very pleased to have him, so he arrived, and every day he went out shooting with us, and as he was a good shot he made a welcome addition to our party. He shot everything he could see, whether it was game or not, but he shot well. We sent all the birds we could not eat up by boat to Manipur for the Sepoys of our escort, who were very grateful for them. We stayed a week the time the Pucca Senna was with us, and he came on afterwards on a tour along the southern boundary of the valley to some very curious places, where they had never seen an English lady before, and where the people exhibited the greatest curiosity and excitement over my advent. We were always coming upon crowds collected at different places on the roads, who had journeyed many miles to see me. They all presented us with a few eggs or fowls, as the case might be, in the hope that the presentation of them would delay us, and that they would be able to get a good view of me. Sometimes, instead of giving us anything, they brought four old women to dance before us, and we would come upon them suddenly over the brow of a hill and find them jumping about on the other side like so many old monkeys for our edification. We were, of course, obliged to stop and look at their exertions, and present them at the end of the performance with rupees. They always came round me and touched my clothes and hands, and seemed to be surprised when I turned up my sleeve and showed them that my arm was white too, like my hands. My clothes caused much curiosity. It was the time then of large dress-improvers, and they had seen me walking out at one village we stopped at in a fashionably-made costume, with at least three steels in it.

The next day I went out on my pony in a riding habit, followed by the usual crowds. We stopped for a few minutes, and I saw our interpreter in fits of laughter over something. I asked my husband what the man was laughing at, and after a little persuasion the interpreter told us that the villagers wished to know what I had done with my tail! At first I had no idea what they meant, but after a little while they explained, and then I discovered that they had imagined the fulness at the back of my dress had concealed a tail, and they could not understand why the habit looked different. We were very much amused, and when we got back to the camp I showed some of them the steels in my dress. They thought it a very funny fashion indeed.

We went away the next day, much to their disappointment, to a place a long way off in the hills, and had a number of queer adventures. The Manipuris told us that this place, called Moombi, was about eighteen miles distant, so we started very early. I commenced by riding, but before we had gone very far the hills became so steep that I got into my long chair and was carried by Nagas. My husband had to walk, and so did Prince Pucca Senna, much to his disgust, as he was a very lazy individual, and never cared to use his legs much. This time there was no help for it, so he puffed and blew as he came up the hill, and said he felt very ill indeed. It must have been thirty miles instead of eighteen, and it was very tiring. I had to hold on to the arms of my chair to keep myself in it at all, and the road got worse and worse, until at last I had to take to my hands and knees too, as by this time the rest of the party were crawling up on all-fours like a string of ants. We got to the top at length, and were going on to the village, which was a few yards ahead, when a message came down from the chief of the village, sent by one of his slaves, saying that if we came any farther he would shoot at us. This was rather alarming at the end of a long and tiring march. The messenger went on to say that they had built a grass hut for us a little below the place we had halted at, and that no one would molest us if we stayed there, but we were not to go into the village. I think if we had had a sufficient armed force with us that my husband would have gone on, but as we were only travelling with a small escort of Manipuris, who seemed much more inclined to run down the hill instead of up it, we agreed to remain in the hut they had built for us, to which we then proceeded. There was no mistake about its being a *grass* hut. It was built of green grass, something like pampas grass, with flowery tops which they had not cut off, but left to wave in a sort of archway over our heads. The roof was very light and airy, and full of large spaces to allow of rain or hail entering the abode if the weather were stormy. The floor was covered with loose, ungainly-looking planks, thrown down anyhow all over it, and if you trod on the end of one suddenly, it started up at the other end like a see-saw. Fortunately we always took a small tent with us to be certain of shelter in case any of the arrangements should fall through, and we had it on this occasion. We soon unpacked it, and got a place on the side of a hill cleared, and began putting it up, hurrying over it as fast as we could, as the clouds were gathering up all round us, and we knew rain was coming. However, long before we had finished erecting it the storm broke. I have rarely seen such a storm.

The wind blew so strongly that it needed all our forces to hold on to the tent-ropes to prevent the whole being blown down the hill on to the top of the unfortunate prince, who, by the way, was housed below us in a wretched grass shed, a copy of ours, only very much smaller. The thunder and lightning were dreadful, as the hills around us re-echoed every peal, and the lightning shone out so vividly in the darkness which had set in. At length the wind went down somewhat, and we adjourned to the hut for dinner, where we sat under one umbrella with our feet on the bath-tub turned upside down, and our plates in our laps. The rain poured meanwhile through the so called roof, and the nodding grass-tops dripped on to our heads. We got to bed about two in the morning, when it cleared up, and the stars came out, as it were, to mock at us for the general soppiness of ourselves and our belongings. We did not dare inquire for the well-being of the prince. Streams of water we knew had rushed down the hill-side, quite powerful enough to carry his hut away.

Next morning very early one of his followers come up to say that his master had not been able to sleep all night, as his house had been swept away and many of his valuables lost; and that he presented his salaams to the Sahib and the Memsahib, and hoped that we did not intend remaining in so horrible a place. It had been our original intention to stay at Moombi three days, but our wet condition, coupled with the hostile reception from the chief, decided us to make a move down the hill. First of all, though, my husband insisted that the chief should come down and pay his respects to us, which, to our great surprise, he did after a little persuasion, bringing his three wives and a number of followers, all of whom were armed with guns of very ancient design, with him. They wore very few clothes, and were not pleasant-looking men, and the women were all very short aud dumpy-looking, and, oh! so dirty. They presented us with eggs and melons, and the wives gave me a curious spear and some baskets of rice. My husband asked them what they meant by greeting us with such an alarming message the night before, to which they replied that they had made a mistake, and did not mean that they would fire on us. We found out afterwards that they thought we were coming to collect some revenue which they had owed to Manipur for some time and refused to pay, and that they were afraid we intended marching into their village and forcing them to pay. My husband hauled the chief (who, by the way, called himself a Rajah) over the coals for it, and told him that he was to come into Manipur, where the revenue case would be inquired into; but we parted very peaceably after going up to the village by the chief's own invitation, where we inspected the outside of his house. It was fenced all round with strong stakes, and on the top of each stake was a head, and more than one of them unmistakably human skulls. Whether the original owners of them had died natural deaths, or whether they were trophies of war, we did not inquire. There were some beautiful elephants' tusks in the chief's veranda, and some fine-toned Kuki gongs, one of which he presented to us. We left with many expressions of affection from the Rajah of Moombi and his wives, but we were very glad when we found ourselves at the foot of the hills leading up to his kingdom, and solemnly made a vow never to return there again. We visited the iron wells on our way home. There are about seven of them, and it was very interesting watching the men at work.

My husband amused himself in the afternoons by teaching the prince English. He used to read out of a queer old spelling-book, filled with words that one would really never use. One sentence was—that is to say, if one could call it a sentence—"an elegant puce quilt." Now, I don't think his highness would ever have used either word, but it amused me greatly to hear him trying to pronounce "quilt"; it developed into "kilt," and never got any farther. I laughed so much that I had to beat a hasty retreat. There was one expression the prince did learn, and that was "good-bye"; but it was a little embarrassing to meet him on arrival and be welcomed by a shake of the hand and a solemn "good-bye." It rather damped one's ardour. He never could understand that it was a farewell salutation, and not a general greeting.

CHAPTER VI.

When we first went to Manipur we had a certain amount of society, as it was then the headquarters of a Ghoorka regiment, which was stationed four miles away from us, at a place called Langthabal; not a pleasant spot by any means, as it had only been roughly cleared for a cantonment, and the roads about it were little better than paths. The officers lived in huts made of bamboo, and the walls had a thin covering of mud on the outside, which some of the more enterprising inmates had painted with whitewash, making them look a little more like the habitations of civilized folks. Some of the huts had very pretty gardens round them, but small, of course, though the flowers there seemed to do twice as well as ours did in the Residency garden. We saw a good deal of the officers in the 44th Ghoorka Rifles, the regiment there when we arrived. They used to come in for polo twice a week, and to what I was pleased to call my "at home" every Thursday, when we played tennis and had the Maharajah's band from four o'clock till six. This band was composed of Nagas, and it was wonderful to hear how easily they learnt English music. Waltzes and any dance music came easiest to them, and they kept excellent time; but they could manage anything, and I have heard them play difficult selections from the great masters without a mistake. Their bandmaster was very talented. As a young man he had gone to Kohima to be taught by the bandmaster of the 44th Ghoorka Rifles, and he had a natural ear for music, and could even sing a little. He used to get very impatient at times when the bandsmen were more stupid than usual, and on one occasion he took to beating them, and they refused to work any longer under him. They were imprisoned, and many of them beaten, but at last, after a great deal of persuasion, backed by a few rupees, they were induced to begin again, and the bandmaster promised to cease from castigating them whenever they played a wrong note.

I shall never forget my first introduction to

the bandmaster. He arrived dressed in what he called his "Calcutta clothes," of which he was immensely proud. They consisted of a white frock coat, made in a very old-fashioned way; black broadcloth continuations, rather short and very baggy; a red-corded silk waistcoat, with large white spots, and tie to match; turn-down collar and ancient top hat, constructed in the year 1800, I fancy. He had a small peony in his button-hole, and last, but not least, patent-leather boots stitched with white and covered with three rows of pearl buttons. He carried a light cane, surmounted by the head and shoulders of a depraved-looking female in oxidized silver as a handle. He showed this to me with great pride, and really it was a marvellous machine, for when you pressed the top of her head, attar of roses came out of her mouth and nose, and if you were anywhere near you were covered with that pungent liquid. It was very difficult to avoid laughing at this curious get-up, and when he had safely embarked on a long overture from "William Tell," I disappeared for a few minutes to give vent to my amusement. He was quite a character, and always afforded me a weekly surprise, as he seldom appeared in the same clothes twice running, and his wardrobe seemed as endless as it was select.

Being able to have the band when we liked was very pleasant. It brought the officers over from Langthabal once a week at any rate, and we always rode out to see them every week. We were very gay there in those days, and we used to have dinner-parties, and I enjoyed the change of going to the mess to dinner now and then. Of course the four miles' journey there was a little trying. The Manipur roads never admitted of driving, so I used to be carried in a long chair by hospital Kahars, and my husband used to ride. It was terribly cold coming back late at night, and often very wet, but we did not mind that very much to get an outing occasionally.

Terribly sorry we were when the decree went forth that we were to lose the regiment. We knew that they might go any day, and a Chin expedition cropped up in the winter of 1888, which took our only neighbours off on the warpath. We were very depressed at the idea of losing them, but perfectly desolated when a letter came saying that we ourselves were to go to another station. We were out in camp when it arrived, and I never shall forget the hopeless silence that fell upon us both at the news. We had counted upon being safely installed at Manipur for three years at the least, but, alas! a number of senior men were coming out from furlough, and had to be provided with districts before the juniors. We had taken so much pride in the place during our ten months' residence there that we were very loath to go. We talked it over, trying to find some way of getting out of leaving, but came to the conclusion there was none. That was in December, but we did not really leave until February, as the officer who was to relieve us had to come a long distance from the other side of the Assam Valley, and he took as long as he possibly could in coming, being as loath to take the place as we were to give it up. Sadly we walked round our gardens, noted the rose-trees only lately arrived from Calcutta, which we had been counting on to make the place beautiful during the coming year, and gazed mournfully at the newly-made asparagus-bed that we hoped would have fed us in three years' time. I almost felt inclined to destroy everything, but my husband was more magnanimous, and even went as far as to say he hoped Mr. Heath (our successor) would enjoy it all.

We made the most of our last two months in Manipur. Two shooting expeditions to the lake, and a journey to Cachar for the Christmas race-meet, occupied most of our remaining time; but, like all things, it came to an end—all too soon for us—and one morning the guns boomed out a salute to our successor. It was a case of "Le roi est mort. Vive le roi!" The same elephants, covered with the same crimson coverings, welcomed him in the identical manner that they had welcomed us. The red-coated Chupprassies hastened to pay their respects to the new Sahib and attend to his wants, heedless of those of the old Sahib, and I think we both felt then what leaving the place would really mean to us. Mr. Heath was much impressed by all the glories prepared for him, but he had not been in the house very long before he told us how much he disliked coming to Manipur. He hadn't a good word to say for it, and I felt very sorry for him, as he really seemed to dread the loneliness terribly. Lonely it certainly was, and the outlook was worse for him than it had been for us, as we had each other, and the regiment was four miles off. He had no one. I knew well how the solitude would weigh on him before many days were over. It had been dreadful work for me at times, when my husband was kept in the office till late in the evening, and I had to amuse myself as best I could from eleven in the morning until dinner-time. There were no books or papers to be got under three weeks or a month's post, and then one had to buy one's books, as there was no going to a library for them. So I felt very sorry for poor Mr. Heath, as he seemed far from strong into the bargain. However, I did my best to cheer him up by taking him all round the gardens and over the house, and showing him that, as far as the place went, he could not wish for a better. Then we went for a walk through the bazaar and on to the polo ground, and eventually, when we returned in the evening, he seemed in a happier frame of mind, and the band playing whilst we were at dinner cheered him up considerably. But next day, when the time came for us to depart, he was very gloomy, and as I was worse myself, I could not put on a pleasant outward appearance. It was very hard to leave the place, having to bid good-bye to all our pets, leaving them in the hands of the servants who might or might not look after them. I took the three little monkeys with me, as I would not part with them, and they were travellers already, as they had come to Manipur with us. My husband did suggest letting them loose in a large grove of mango-trees not far from the Residency that was filled with monkeys which we often used to go and feed with rice and plantains, but I knew how they fought amongst themselves, and how the big ones bullied the little ones, so I preferred taking my three with us. I took a last walk round the grounds, and almost directly after breakfast our horses came to the door and we had to make a start. All the servants that were remaining behind came and bid us good-bye, and some of the red-coated Chupprassies gave us little presents of dried fruits and nuts. We rode out of the place very slowly, but as soon as the quarter-guard gates had closed behind us we put our ponies into a gallop, and never stopped till three or four miles lay between us and the Residency, and neither of us spoke much for the rest of the ten that limited our journey that day.

We were going to a place over two hundred miles away called Jorehat, in the Assam Valley, near the Brahmapootra, and to get to it we had to pass through Kohima, in the Naga Hills, ninety-six miles from Manipur. It was my first visit there, and I enjoyed the eight days' journey to it immensely. We were accompanied as far as Mao Thana (the boundary between the Manipur state and Kohima) by the eldest son of the Tongal General. Before going on, I think some description of the latter officer will not be amiss, especially as he has played so important a part in the late rebellion. He was an old man, nearer eighty than seventy I should think, taller than the average Manipuri, and marvellously active for his age. He had a fine old face, much lined and wrinkled with age and the cares of state which had fallen upon him when he was quite a young man, and had in no wise lessened as his years increased. He had piercing black eyes, shaggy overhanging white eyebrows, and white hair. His nose was long and slightly hooked, and his mouth was finely cut and very determined.

He was fond of bright colours, and I never remember seeing him in anything but a delicate pink silk dhotee, a dark coat made from a first-rate English pattern, and a pink turban, and when the orchids were in bloom, he seldom appeared without a large spray of some gorgeous-hued specimen in the top of his turban. The Tongal always reminded me of an eagle. He had the same keen, rugged expression and deep-set, glowing eyes. Few things happened without his knowledge and consent, and if he withheld his approbation from any matter, there would invariably be a hitch in it somewhere. He was credited with more bloodshed than any man in the kingdom. If a village had misbehaved itself, raided on another, or refused to pay revenue or do Lalup, the Tongal would travel out to that village and wipe it off the face of the earth. Men, women, and children were cut down without the slightest compunction. Few escaped, and these travelled away and joined other villages; but every house and barn and shed was burnt, pigs and fowls destroyed, and ruin and devastation reigned where prosperity and plenty had held sway before. I believe in later years restrictions were brought to bear upon the Manipur durbar which prevented such wholesale slaughter; but in earlier days the Tongal had, as he expressed it, "nautched through many villages" in the style described, and brought desolation into many a hillman's peaceful home. If he had his faults, he had his virtues. He was very enterprising, fond of building bridges, and improving the roads about the capital. Like the Senaputti, he was a keen soldier, enjoyed watching good shooting, and had been in his younger days a first-rate shot himself. He was an obstinate old man, and it was very difficult to get him to listen to any proposition if it did not please him at the outset; but when once he had promised to get anything done, he did not go back from his word, and one knew it was reliable. He lived in a large house some distance to the south of the palace, with his family. Of these, only two sons were of any importance—the eldest, called Yaima, and the second son, a very handsome young fellow, named Lumphel Singh. The latter was perhaps the most influential, and my husband always said he thought that he would take his father's place in the state when anything happened to the old man. Lumphel was the favourite aide-de-camp of the Maharajah, and he was the officer in charge of the hundred and twenty-eight miles of road between Manipur and Cachar. At durbars he used to stand behind the Maharajah's chair with a very magnificent uniform covered with gold lace, and a gold turban.

Yaima, the eldest brother, was not good-looking at all, but a nice young fellow, and very hardworking. He came with us on our journey to Kohima at the time of which I write, and was very obliging, and ready to put himself out in any way in order that we might be comfortable, which, considering that we were departing, as we then thought, for good from the place, was very courteous on his part. We were very sorry to part with him at Mao Thana. The scenery on the road between Kohima and Manipur is magnificent. Some of the hills run as high as nine thousand feet, and yet until you are within three days' journey of Kohima the road is almost level, winding in and out along a narrow valley. Forests of oak abound the whole way, and in the cold weather the trees lose their foliage, making it look very English-like and wintry. Sometimes you find yourself riding along a narrow path which skirts round the side of a steep hill, while below you is the river, clear and blue and deep, with an occasional rapid disturbing the calm serenity of its flow. The hills around are studded with villages, and peopled by various tribes. The Nagas in the immediate vicinity of Kohima are perhaps a finer race than any hillmen to be found in Assam. They are called Ungamis, and are very fine men, most of them six feet high at least, broad shouldered, and powerfully built. Their dress is curious, and quite different to any of the Nagas about Manipur. It consists of a kind of very short kilt made of coarse black cloth, trimmed with three or four rows of shells like cowries. In old days, before Kohima was as settled and quiet as it is in these days, these rows of shells are said to have borne a meaning —a man who had never taken a human head was not allowed to sew them on to his kilt. For every head taken they affixed so many cowries, five or six at a time, as the case might be, and a warrior with three rows on his kilt was considered a great gun indeed.

The Mao Nagas were Ungamis, and used to

be rather a handful for the Manipuris to manage. They were always getting up feuds with the villagers over the border, and the Manipuris were very often afraid of hauling them over the coals for it, for fear of getting the worst of the fray. We stayed two days at Kohima on our way to Jorehat, and travelled after leaving there through the Namba forest to the next station, called Golaghat. We took eight days to do this bit of our journey, as the weather was delicious, and we wanted to make the most of our time on the road, being in no hurry to arrive at our destination. This Namba forest covers an enormous area. It extends hundreds of miles each side of the road, which is constructed right through the middle of it. The scenery is wonderful. High forest jungle rises each side of you as you ride along. Here and there you come across a river, whose sandy banks show the footprints of many a wild beast. Bears, tigers, leopards, and elephants swarm in the jungle around, but one seldom sees anything more exciting than a harmless deer browsing by the wayside, or a troop of long-tailed monkeys crossing the road. It is all very wild and beautiful, and when we eventually came to the end of our eight days' march through the Namba, and reached cultivated regions once more, we were quite sorry. We stayed two days at Golaghat, the first station reached after leaving the forest, and then proceeded to our new subdivision, arriving there at the end of three days.

CHAPTER VII.

THERE is no necessity to give a detailed account of the time spent between our leaving Manipur and our return there. It extended over a period of some ten or twelve weeks only. Instead of remaining at Jorehat three months as we had at first expected, we were there only ten days, just long enough to get everything unpacked and stowed away, when a telegram came from Shillong, ordering my husband to another station called Gaùhati, on the Brahmapootra. As it was a better appointment, he accepted it, but it was very hard work having to start off on the march again before we had had time to rest ourselves after our long journey from Manipur. That wonderful domestic whom we could never do without in India, the bearer, soon repacked all our things. Why haven't we someone like a bearer in England? He is a perfect godsend in the shiny East. He is valet to the Sahib, makes the beds, dusts the rooms, cleans the lamps and boots, and is responsible for all the performances of the other domestics. If they fail to do their duty, or break your furniture or crockery, you scold the bearer. If one of your horses goes lame or gets out of condition, the bearer knows of it very soon, and if your cook sends you up anything nasty for dinner, or the butter is sour or the milk turned, your bearer is admonished. No doubt he lectures the other servants for their misdeeds, and takes many gratuities from them, varying in bulk, for pacifying his irate master or mistress. He generally gets on amicably with the whole establishment, but sometimes he makes an enemy of one or other of the servants, and ructions are as constant as they are noisy. The two bearers (for they generally hunt in couples) that we had had been with my husband for many years. They were both very excellent servants, though the elder of the two gave himself the airs and graces of a Maharajah.

My advent into the menage did not please him at all. Well he knew that his little sins of omission and commission, so easily perpetrated in a bachelor establishment, would all vanish and be things of the past when a Memsahib came out from Belat* to rule the roost. Many a battle have I had with Mr. Moni Ram Dass, as my husband's chief factotum was called, before I could get him to see that my way was not his way sometimes. For instance, on one occasion shortly after my arrival in India I found him airing the *whole* of my husband's wardrobe in my drawing-room at an hour when visitors were certainties. Now, there are some garments in a man's outfit —and in a woman's, too, for that matter—which, with the best intention in the world, could never be made to look fitting ornaments for a lady's drawing-room. I expounded this theory to the bearer on this occasion, but it was some time before I got him clearly to understand that his master's wardrobe was to be confined to the limits of the dressing-room and back veranda; and when he did carry off the garments in question, it was with an expression on his face of severe displeasure at my want of taste in not considering them in the light of ornaments to my drawing-room. One virtue in this estimable in-

* Belat—England.

dividual certainly was worthy of all praise: he knew how to pack.

When we were leaving Manipur, he had packed all our belongings, and on our arrival at Jorehat, after a long, rough journey, we found everything in perfect order, and not even a cup broken. He repacked our things when we had to leave there again, and took them himself to Gauhati, saving us all the trouble of having to look after our heavy baggage ourselves, and enabling us to follow on in comfort some days later.

It was beginning to be hot when we arrived at Gauhati early in April, and I dreaded having to spend the hot season in the plains. It was to be my first experience of great heat, as the summer before in Manipur we had never needed punkahs, and on the hottest day we ever had, the thermometer registered only 87°.

A week after we went to Gauhati, news came from Manipur that Mr. Heath, our successor, was very ill indeed with dysentery. And as every day went by, bringing reports of his condition, sometimes better, and then worse again, we began to fear that he would not recover. At last one day a telegram came saying that all was over, and that he had died the previous evening. We were both very sorry to hear it. We had liked what we saw of him so much, and had been so sorry to leave him there, apart from our own sad feelings at going, knowing that he disliked and dreaded the place so much. It seemed terribly sad. I knew well, too, that it would mean our returning there, and much as I had regretted leaving, I did not want to go back.

I cannot tell why the dislike had arisen within me at the thoughts of returning; but the journey was so long, and the time of year so trying, and on the top of that there was the feeling that a man whom we had known and liked had just died in the house, and that if we went back it would be to rooms that were full of his things, and associations quite unlike those we had left behind us. Maybe that a warning of all that was yet to come filled me with some unknown presentiment of evil, but it seemed as though our return there was inevitable.

Within twenty-four hours after we had heard of Mr. Heath's death came the letter offering Manipur again to my husband. I watched his face light up as he read it, full of eagerness to get back to the place he loved, and I knew that I could never tell him that I did not want him to go. My reasons for not wishing to return seemed childish, and I thought he would not understand the superstitious ideas which filled me with dread at the idea of going back. So when he came to me with the letter and asked me to decide whether we should say yes or no to it, I said we had better accept what it offered.

As it was so late in the year for travelling, and the weather so hot and unhealthy, my husband decided to leave me in Shillong on his way to Manipur, and let me fellow in October. It was with a heavy heart that I superintended the arrangements for the return journey. An undefinable dread seemed to predominate over all I did, and I bid good-bye to my husband when he left me behind in Shillong with a very heavy heart, and my anxiety was not lessened when I heard from him day after day, giving me terrible accounts of all he was going through on the way. Every one of his servants, with the exception of the Khitmutghar, got ill with fever and other complaints peculiar to the time of year. They had to be carried the whole way, and my husband had to cook his own dinner and groom his horses himself every day, besides having to unpack all the necessary tables and chairs at each halting-place, and do them up again before starting off next morning. It was only a mercy that he did not get ill himself to add to the other miseries, and that I was not there to make extra work for him. Very glad was I to hear from him at last that he had arrived safely at Manipur. I don't think he felt very bright at first. He was quite alone there. The regiment was still away in the Chin Hills, and rumours were afloat that when it did return most of the men were to be drafted to Shillong, and only a wing left to garrison Langthabal. My husband complained, too, that the Residency had somewhat gone to seed since we left. During Mr. Heath's illness and the time which elapsed between his death and our return the servants had all taken a holiday, so there was a good deal to be done to get things into order again. Several rooms in the house that contained the dead man's effects were kept locked up, and it was some time before my husband could get the whole house opened and the things sent away down to Calcutta.

Meanwhile I was enjoying myself very much, having got over my first feelings of loneliness, and made friends with everyone in the place, more or less. Shillong is a lovely little station nestling away amongst the Khasia Hills, in the midst of pine woods, and abounding in waterfalls and mountain-torrents. The climate is delicious all the year round, and the riding and driving as good, if not better, than any hill-station in India. Life there was very pleasant, not a superabundance of gaiety, but quite enough to be enjoyable. I have spent some very happy days there with some good friends, many of whom, alas! I can never hope to see again; and the memories that come to me of Shillong and my sojourn there are tinged with sadness and regret, even though those days were good and pleasant while they lasted.

Things have changed there now, that is, as far as the comings and goings of men change, but the hills remain the same, and the face of Nature will not alter. Her streams will whisper to the rocks and flowers of all that has been and that is to be. So runs the world. Where others lived and loved, sorrowed and died, two hundred years ago, we are living now, and when our day is over and done there will be others to take our place, until a time comes when there shall be no more change, neither sorrow nor death, and the former things shall have passed away for ever.

CHAPTER VIII.

I LEFT Shillong early in November, 1889, travelling part of the way towards Manipur quite alone, and had a terrible experience too. I had arranged to journey a distance of thirty-eight miles in one day. I sent one of my horses on the day before, and started in a "Khasia Thoppa" down the last hill of the range upon which Shillong is situated, which brings you down into the plain of Sylhet. A Thoppa is a very curious mode of locomotion. It is a long cane basket, with a seat in the middle, from which hangs a small board to rest your feet upon. Over your head is a covered top made of cane, covered with a cloth. You sit in this basket and a man carries you on his back, supporting some of the weight by tying a strap woven of cane on to the back of the Thoppa, which he puts over his forehead. The Khasias, luckily, are very strong men, but they think it necessary always to begin by informing you that you are much too heavy to be lifted by any single individual, unless that said individual be compensated at the end of the journey with double pay.

You ask him what you weigh, and he scratches an excessively dirty head, shuts up one eye, spits a quantity of horrible red fluid out of his mouth, and then informs you that he should put you down as eighteen or nineteen stone, and he even will go as far as twenty sometimes. This, to a slim, elegant-looking person, partakes of the nature of an insult, but eventually he picks you up on his back and proceeds along the road with you as fast as he can, as if you were a feather weight. Going along backwards, and knowing that, should the man's headstrap break, the chances are you will be precipitated down the Khud,* are certainly not pleasurable sensations; but it is astonishing how exceedingly callous you become after a lengthy course of Thoppa rides up in the hills. Sometimes your Thoppa wallah** may be slightly inebriated, when he will lurch about in a horrible manner, emit a number of

* Khud—precipice, cliff.

** Thoppa wallah—bearer, or man who carries Thoppas.

curious gurgling noises from the depths of his throat, and eventually tumble down in the centre of the road, causing you grievous hurt.

At other times he will take into consideration that it is a cold night, the Memsahib is going to a Nautch,* and will be there four of five hours, while he is left to his own reflections outside, waiting to carry her home again when her festivites have subsided. Having arrived at the conclusion that the cold will probably by that time be intense, he will come to take you to the scene of action enveloped in every covering that he can get together. After he has carried you a short way he begins getting hot, and rapidly divests himself of his many wrappers, placing them on the top of your machine, where they flutter about, hitting you now and then playfully in the mouth or eye, as the case may be, and making themselves as generally unpleasant as they possibly can. Having done so, they end by falling off into the road. Your Khasia perceives them, and immediately descends with you on to his hands and knees, and grovels about until he recovers the

* Nautch—ball.

fallen raiment. During this process your head assumes a downward tendency, and your heels fly heavenwards; and should you move in anyway ever so slightly, you immediately find yourself sitting on the ground in a more hasty than dignified attitude, upbraiding your Khasia in English. You may swear at a native and abuse all his relations, as their custom is, in his own language, and you will not impress him in any way; but use good sound fish-wife English, and he will treat you as a person worthy of respect.

On my journey from Shillong, at the time of which I write, I fell in with two very amiable Khasias. One could speak Hindostanee rather well, and he walked beside me as I travelled down the hill and talked to me on various interesting subjects. He asked me a great deal about the Lushais, and I invented some wonderful anecdotes for his delectation. When we parted, I think I had impressed him with the idea that I was a person of great moral worth.

At the foot of the hill I got into a small train, the only railway to be found at present in that side of Assam. I think it only extends over about twelve miles of country, and there are about four trains, two up and two down daily. They do not trouble themselves by putting on too much speed. We, my servants and I, travelled as far as we could in it, and then I found myself within twenty miles of Sylhet—my proposed destination—in lots of time to ride in comfortably before dark, and get my servants and baggage in at the same time. But, alas! the inevitable fate of the traveller in Sylhet was destined to be mine, too, on this occasion; and when I got out of the train, expecting to find my coolies waiting for me, I found a wretched police inspector, who informed me that the coolies had all run away, and he could not get me any more. What was to be done I knew not, but after some delay I met a young fellow whom I knew slightly, as he was connected with the railway, and I had seen him passing through the district once before. He was a perfect godsend to me on this occasion, and after some hours' hunting for coolies he managed to get the requisite number, and started them off with my luggage.

The next thing to be done was to start myself. Mr. A—— kindly offered to go with me half-way, as it was then four o'clock, and only two hours of daylight left. Off we started, he on the most extraordinary pony I have ever seen, that looked as though it might fall down at any moment, and I on a small Manipuri pony I had taken with me up in the hills. We started off galloping, and went as hard as we could for six miles. I hoped that about seven miles from Sylhet I should find a pony-trap waiting for me which a planter had offered to send to meet me, so I did not spare my small steed, as I knew he would not think anything of twelve miles.

By the time we got to the river, where I expected the cart to meet me, it was almost dark. My poor pony was terribly tired and hot, but Mr. A——'s curious old beast seemed none the worse. We crossed the river on a ferry, and then found there was no cart on the opposite side. It was a terrible blow, for our ponies had done enough as it was. Night was rapidly overtaking us, and seven miles of the road lay before us to be got over somehow. I had passed all my coolies three miles away on the road from the railway, and knew that they would not be in for hours. There was nothing to be done but to go on as best we could. There were tracks of the cart-wheels in the road, so I knew it had been there, and it made it all the more annoying. It was no good trying to gallop on, as my pony was so tired he could scarcely crawl.

We proceeded slowly for about two miles. It was getting darker every minute, and at length we could see nothing at all, but knew that we had still five more weary miles to travel over. Mr. A—— suggested our urging our horses into a canter, which ended disastrously for me, as my pony caught his foot in something on the road and landed on his head. That was the end of all idea of riding, so I got off, hauled him up on his legs by dint of much persuasion, and started off walking. The road was ankle-deep in loose sand, jackals hurried by us at every moment, and noises startled me at every turn. At last I remembered that the planter who had sent the cart out lived somewhere in that neighbourhood. When we had been quartered in Sylhet, I had often ridden past his house, though I had never been actually up to it, and I told Mr. A—— that I thought we had better steer for his bungalow, if we could only find the road up to it. We went on as fast as we could, considering, and at length saw the lights of the house standing some distance to our left away from the road.

The next thing was to find the way up to it. My companion asked me to look after the ponies —a rather unnecessary precaution, as they were too tired to need any looking after—and he proceeded to try and find the road. After a little while I heard a stifled call in the distance, which was repeated, and then I discovered that poor Mr. A—— had fallen into a horribly wet, slushy rice-field, and needed my help to extricate him. Having given him the necessary aid, and hauled him out, we decided that any more searching for the road up to the house would be a futile waste of energy, and were preparing to make the best of our way into Sylhet, when a coolie woman came by, and we rushed at her and asked if she could show us the way to the Sahib's bungalow. She seemed very much alarmed at our sudden appearance, as we were then only dimly visible by the light of the rising moon. However, she said after a little that she would not mind conveying us up to the house, provided that we would allow her a fair start in front of us, as she professed to be much alarmed at our horses.

We proceeded slowly and solemnly behind her, and at length found ourselves not at the bungalow, but at the tea-house, an erection made of corrugated iron in which the tea was manufactured. All round this building there were wire stays which were fastened in the ground and attached to the roof, to prevent the latter being blown off in storms of wind. My poor tired pony caught his feet in one of these wires and tumbled down; so, thinking that it was better to take what rest he could, he did not trouble himself to get up again. It was not much good scolding our guide, but we seemed no better off than we had been in the road below, and the lights of the bungalow gleamed just as far away as before. Mr. A—— suggested shouting, so simultaneously we all lifted up our voices and shouted as loud as we could.

At length, after doing this a great many times, a light appeared in the door of the bungalow; and a few minutes afterwards the figure of my friend the planter became visible descending the hill upon which his house was situated, and coming armed with a big stick to see what evil spirits were in possession of his tea-house.

Very much surprised was he when he found there was a lady in the case, and not a little disconcerted over his own appearance, as he was not clad in raiment suitable to the entertaining of female visitors.

I was much too tired, however, to notice whether he was got up for the occasion or not, and he seemed a perfect godsend to us both after all we had gone through.

He soon took us up to his house, and in half an hour gave us dinner. Real dinner, too—not a shadowy make-belief; but soup, entrée, and joint, just as though we had come by invitation, and this had been the result of some days' preparation.

How we did eat! There was little doubt that we appreciated the excellent fare set before us, and at the end of it I felt a different being.

Our friend the planter had meanwhile got himself up regardless of expense, and offered to drive me into Sylhet, an offer which I most gladly accepted, leaving the poor Jabberwock in a comfortable stable, with a large bundle of grass in front of him, which he was too tired to eat.

We did not take long to get over the four miles to Sylhet, where I bade farewell to the planter and Mr. A——, who returned with him to the garden.

I had the pleasure of lying down on a bed with no bedding, and waiting until my coolies and baggage should arrive, with part of my muddy habit rolled up to serve for a pillow; and very well I slept for three good hours, when at two o'clock in the morning my goods and chattels commenced dropping in, and I was able to go to bed in real, sober earnest.

Next morning the Jabberwock arrived, looking rather miserable, with a very large swelling on his leg, and a bad girthgall; so there was no possibility of our continuing our journey that day, as the servants all said they were dying, and could not move on at any price. However, the day following they recovered sufficiently to proceed another fifteen miles; and after three more days I arrived at Cachar, where I found my husband, who had come down from Manipur to meet me.

CHAPTER IX.

It was strange finding myself back in Manipur after nearly nine months' absence; but though the house had had several improvements made to it, and the grounds were prettier than when we had left in February, I could not settle down in the place as I had done before. Poor Mr. Heath was buried in our own garden, quite close to the house—so close, in fact, that I could see his grave from my bedroom window. There had been two graves there before—one was Major Trotter's, who was once political agent at Manipur, and died there from wounds which he had received fighting in Burmah; the other was that of a young Lieutenant Beavor, who had also died at the Residency, of fever. But we had never known either of these two men, so that I did not look upon them in the same light as I did on Mr. Heath, and his sudden, sad death seemed to haunt me. Once a friend of mine remarked to my husband, "What an unlucky place Manipur is! I have seen so many political agents go up there, and something always seems to happen to them." Hearing this gave me a cold shudder, and I longed to get my husband to give up a place so associated with gloomy incidents, and take some other district in the province. Not that I was ever really afraid of anything tangible.

I rode alone all over the country, fearing nothing from the inhabitants, who knew me, and would have been only too ready to help me had I needed aid; and I have been left for days together quite alone at the Residency while my husband had to be out in camp. Once he had to go down to Tammu in Burmah, five days' journey from Manipur, and I was too ill to go with him, so stayed behind.

For sixteen days I was there all alone. We had no neighbours nearer than a hundred miles off, and I never even heard English spoken until my husband returned. The old ayah used to sleep on my doormat at night, and I always had sentries outside the house, back and front. I used to hear, or imagine I heard, all kinds of noises sometimes, and get up, waking the old woman from her noisy slumbers to come and do a midnight parade all round the house, searching in every nook and corner for the disturber of my rest, which was probably nothing more harmful than an antiquated bat roaming about in the roof, or a rat in the cellars beneath the house. The poor old ayah used to pretend to be very valiant on these occasions, and carefully hunt in every dark corner which I had already turned out; but she was always glad to get back when the search was ended to her own venerable blanket, in which she used to roll her attenuated form, and snore away the long vigils of the nights.

Poor old Moonia! she was a faithful old soul, and has tramped many a mile after me in my wanderings backwards and forwards. She was a lazy old woman, but if I told her so, she gave me warning on the spot. She did this very frequently—on an average, six times a month; but after a little I got accustomed to it—in fact, I may say I got rather to like it—and I never by any chance reminded her of her promised flitting, or took any notice of the warning when she gave it to me. She was a very quarrelsome old creature, and had some very bitter enemies. First and above all she detested the head bearer. She hated him with a deep and deadly hatred, and if she could do him a bad turn she would do it, even though it caused her much fatigue, bodily and mental, to accomplish it. Next to the bearer she disliked the wife of one of the Chupprassies. This female was a powerfully-built Naga woman, with a very good opinion of herself; and she returned the ayah's dislike most fully. They were always at war, and on one occasion they had a stand-up fight. We had gone out into camp, and as Moonia (the ayah) had not been well, I left her at home instead of taking her with me, as I generally did. Two days after we had started, a report reached us that she had had a terrible fight with the Chupprassie's wife, and the latter had injured her very seriously. We heard nothing more about it at that time, so I imagined that the ayah's wounds were healing, and that I should not be informed as to details at all. Not so, however. We returned to the Residency a fortnight later, and I sent for my abigail as usual, receiving in return a message saying that she could not come, as she was still dangerously ill. Having, however, insisted on her appearing, she came—very slowly, and with her head so enveloped in coverings that I could not see even the tip of her nose. Groans issued forth at intervals, and she subsided on to the floor directly she entered the room. After a little parleying, I persuaded her to undo her various blankets, and show me the extent of her injuries. They were not serious, and the only real wound was one on the top of her head, which certainly was rather a deep cut. However, I soon impressed upon her that I did not think she was as near death's door as she evidently imagined, and let her return to her own apartments, vowing vengeance on her adversary.

Moonia presented a petition soon afterwards, and my husband had to try the case, which he proceeded to do in the veranda of the Residency. The evidence was very conflicting. All the complainant's witnesses bore testimony against her, and *vice-versâ;* and the language of the principal parties concerned was very voluble and abusive. The ayah made a great sensation, however, by producing the log of wood she had been beaten with, covered with hair and blood, and the clothes she had worn at the time, in a similar gory condition. The hair in the stick was very cleverly arranged. Where it had originally come from was not easy to define; but it was stuck in bunches the whole length of the stick, and must have been a work of time and ingenuity. However, there were many exclamations of commiseration for the complainant, and eventually the defendant was fined one rupee, and bound over to keep the peace.

Then ensued a funny scene. The ayah argued that the fine imposed was not heavy enough, and the adversary threatened her with more violence as soon as she should leave the presence of the Sahib; and they swore gaily at each other, as only two native women know how to swear, and had to be conveyed from the court in different directions by a small guard of the 43rd Ghoorkas, who were mightily amused at the whole business. I thought at the time that should the Chupprassie's wife ever get an opportunity of wreaking vengeance on the ayah, she was just the sort of woman to make that revenge a deep one; and I pitied the ayah if she ever fell into her hands. The day did come before very long; but of that I shall speak later on.

Our Chupprassies were very useful, but very lazy, and puffed up with pride in their own loveliness. Their red coats with the "V.R." buttons, covered with gold braid, lent them much dignity; and there were many little offices which they absolutely refused to perform because they wore the Queen's livery, and considered themselves too important. For instance, I requested four of them once to go into the garden and catch grasshoppers out of the long grass with which to feed a cage full of little birds. One of the four alone condescended to go; the rest solemnly refused, saying that they could not demean themselves by such a performance, and that I must get the Naga boys out of the village to do it for them. And I had to give in to them ignominiously.

These ten Chupprassies were all supposed to be interpreters of some kind or another; but for the most part they could speak no other dialect but their own, whatever that happened to be, and had no idea of translating it into any other tongue.

Altogether, they were decidedly more ornamental than useful. Two of them rode extremely well, and they acted as my jockeys in some pony-races which the Senaputti got up one Christmas Day, amongst other sports, for the amusement of our Sepoys and his own.

The Senaputti had got the idea of this Gymkhana from having seen the 44th Ghoorka sports on one occasion at Langthabal, when that regiment was stationed there, and besides the ordinary races and competitions, the Manipuris had some which I have never seen anywhere else. One feat they performed was to lay a man on the top of six bayonets. The bayonets were fixed to the rifles, and the latter were then driven into the ground like stakes with the points upwards. A man then lay down flat on the ground and made himself as stiff as possible, when he was lifted up by four other men, and laid along the tops of the bayonets. Had he moved they must have gone into him, and we never knew how the performance was managed, or whether they fixed anything on the points of the bayonets to prevent their piercing his flesh; but it did not look a nice trick at all, and one always dreaded an accident. There was wrestling, too, in which the princes took part, and foot races, and the Senaputti gave the prizes, mostly in money. And to wind up there was a play. The Maharajah had three jesters, exactly like the old English fashion of having court-jesters to amuse royalty.

The Manipuri specimens were very funny indeed. Their heads were shaved like the back of a poodle, with little tufts of hair left here and there; and their faces were painted with streaks of different-coloured paints, and their eyebrows whitened. They wore very few clothes, but what they had were striped red and green and a variety of shades. They walked up to the tent where we were sitting to watch the sports, all leaning against each other, and carrying on a lively conversation in Manipuri, which seemed to amuse the spectators very much. On reaching the door of the tent they all fell down at our feet, making terrible grimaces by way of greeting, and then they picked each other up and retired a few yards off and commenced the performance. One disguised himself as an old woman, and another as a native doctor, and the third as a sick man, lying on the ground covered with a white sheet. Someone out of the crowd was impressed into the play, and he had to call the doctor to the sick man, who was meanwhile heaving up and down upon the ground in a very extraordinary manner. The doctor came and poked him about, making observations in Manipuri, at which everyone roared with laughter; and then the old woman arrived and dragged the doctor off home. She was supposed to be his wife, and as soon as she appeared a scuffle ensued, in which the old woman's clothes fell off. We thought best to beat a retreat, as the play was beginning to be rowdy and the dialogue vulgar; but I believe that it went on for some hours afterwards, as we heard shouts of laughter proceeding from the direction of the polo-ground, where the sports were held, late at night; and the princes told us the next day that it had been a very good play, and the only pity was that we had witnessed so little of it.

CHAPTER X.

All was peaceful at Manipur around us until September 11, 1890. As day after day went by, we seemed to get to know the royal family better. Rumours of strife amongst the brothers reached us from time to time, and petty jealousies showed themselves in some of their dealings —jealousies that the weak will ever have for the strong, in whatever country or community it may be. But we were good friends with them all, though it was difficult at times to avoid giving cause for disputes between the Pucca Senna and his more powerful brother, the Senaputti. If one came more often than the other, that other would get annoyed, and refuse to come at all for some time. The Pucca Senna got very angry, because the Senaputti frequently escorted the young princesses on their visits to me, and on one occasion he tried to arrest some of their attendants in the road when they were leaving the Residency, which might have been the beginning of a very serious disturbance, had not my husband, hearing privately that something of the kind was meditated, sent an orderly and a Chupprassie with the girls to see them safely as far as the palace.

The Senaputti had left the Residency on that occasion some time before the young princesses went away. Poor children! they were very much alarmed at the attempt to waylay their attendants, and it was a very long time before they summoned up enough courage to pay us another visit.

We knew that the Pucca Senna and the Senaputti were rivals, too. Both wished to marry a girl who was supposed to be the most beautiful woman in Manipur. She rejoiced in the name of Maïpâkbi, but I never thought her as pretty as some of the young princesses who used to come and see me. She was not a royalty herself, but was the daughter of a wealthy goldsmith who lived near the palace; her father was a prominent member of the Maharajah's durbar, or council. She was taller, though, than the average Manipuri, about sixteen years of age, and very fair, with quantities of long black hair. She was always very well dressed, and had a great many gold bracelets on her arms, and some necklaces of pure gold which weighed an enormous amount.

"Fine feathers make fine birds," says an old proverb, and in this case it was certainly true; but the two princes thought her beautiful, and were at daggers drawn about her. We had a big nautch one night, to which Maïpiâkbi came as chief dancer. All the princes were there to see it, and the two rivals for the young lady's affections sat one on each side of me. The Senaputti was all cheerfulness and good-humour, but the Pucca Senna was very gloomy and morose, and at the end of the evening my husband said we must never ask the two brothers together again. Shortly afterwards we heard that they had had a terrible quarrel, in which the Maharajah had taken the part of the Pucca Senna, and that the Senaputti had sworn never to speak to the latter again, an oath which he kept to the letter.

Meanwhile I went away to the hills, and all seemed to go on quietly for two or three months, though a storm was brewing in the meanwhile, which only needed an opportunity to burst forth and overwhelm the reigning power in destruction. The eight brothers split up into two factions—the Maharajah, Pucca Senna, Samoo Hengeba, and the Dooloroi Hengeba formed one side; whilst the Jubraj, Senaputti, Angao Senna, and the young Zillah Singh all leagued together. Of the first four named, the Samoo Hengeba and the Dooloroi Hengeba are the two that have not been mentioned previously. The first of these was the officer in charge of the Maharajah's elephants, numbering about sixty. It was his duty to manage all the arrangements in connection with them, and on grand occasions, when the Maharajah rode on an elephant, his brother, the Samoo Hengeba, acted as Mahout.* The name means Chief over elephants, Samoo being the Manipuri name for an elephant, and Hengeba head or chief.

The Dooloroi Hengeba had command of all the Maharaja's doolies.** This mode of travelling was confined to the rich, and was con-

* Mahout—driver.

** Doolies—a sort of palanquin, made of cane, in which people are carried.

sidered a mark of great dignity; not everyone could indulge in this luxury, and those who did had to get special permission to use them, though sometimes they were conferred upon ministers of state by the Maharajah as a mark of recognition for their services. The Maharajah seldom travelled in any other style, as he was a very stout, apoplectic kind of personage, and it suited him better to be carried than to ride or go on an elephant. His dooly was a very magnificent affair, made of wood, with gilt hangings all round it, and a gilt top, which could be put over it in wet weather.

Prince Angao Senna was in charge of the road between Burmah and Manipur. He was supposed to travel up and down it to see that it was kept in a state of repair, but I don't think he ever did so. He was quite young, about two or three and twenty, and I never remember seeing him without his having a large piece of betel-nut in his mouth, which he used to chew. It gave him the appearance of having a swollen face, as he stuffed enormous bits of it into his mouth all at once, exactly as a monkey will do with nuts or anything of the kind, and people said he never cared for anything but eating and drinking and watching pigeon-fights.

The Manipuris are great gamblers, and they used to make these pigeon-fights the occasion for betting considerably. A good fighting pigeon was worth a lot of money—forty or fifty rupees. They were handsome birds, larger than the ordinary pigeon sold in the market for an anna apiece, and they had most beautiful plumage. The contests between two of them were generally held in the middle of one of the principal roads. Each owner brought his pigeon to the scene of action tied up in a cloth, and they were then put under a wicker cage, something like a hen-coop, where they fought until one conquered.

It was very unexciting to watch it, we thought; but the crowd of spectators used to take a breathless interest in the combatants, and bet considerably upon them. I never quite understood how they decided which bird had won, as they simply beat each other with their wings, cooing loudly the whole time, and sometimes one seemed victorious, and sometimes the other. However, there were doubtless points in the combat which we did not understand, and the Manipuris always took the deepest interest in them.

Latterly, after the expulsion of the Mahărajah, his brother, the regent, put a stop to these pigeon-fights, as the gambling over them was becoming excessive, and several of the younger princes had been seriously involved, and the state had had to pay their debts. A heavy punishment was inflicted upon anyone found encouraging a pigeon-fight, and even the casual spectators received a beating, whilst the owners of the birds, and whoever had instigated the proceedings, were hauled up before the durbar and fined large sums. However, Prince Angao Senna was never caught red-handed, though we heard that he still continued to encourage and attend these séances on the quiet.

June, July, and August went by. Day by day came letters from my husband at Manipur full of all the little details which went to make up his life there, and never a dream of future trouble arose to disturb our peace of mind. The only thing that rather worried my husband was the approaching departure of our only neighbour, an officer in the 44th Ghoorkas, quartered at that time at Langthabal. Since the regiment had left in the winter of 1888 for Burmah, we had never had more than a wing of it back at Langthabal, and in the winter of 1889 it was decided that the troops should be removed altogether, and our escort increased from sixty to a hundred men under a native officer. But this decision took some time to effect. Barracks had to be built in our grounds for the accommodation of extra men, and these took time in building. So that it was not until January, 1891, that the garrison at Langthabal departed.

CHAPTER XI.

EARLY in September, 1890, the storm that had long been gathering amongst the princes at Manipur came to a head and burst. The spark that kindled the blaze arose out of a very small matter indeed. The young prince Zillah Singh had been quarrelling with the Pucca Senna over everything and anything that could be found to quarrel about, and at length the Pucca Senna got the Maharajah to forbid Zillah Singh to sit in the durbar, at the same time depriving him of some small offices of state which he usually performed.

The young prince lost no time in consulting with his powerful brother and ally, the Senaputti. The result was that one night, about midnight, when the Maharajah had retired and the rest of the palace was wrapped in slumber, the young prince collected a handful of followers, and with his brother Angao Senna climbed the wall leading to the Maharajah's apartments, and began firing off rifles into the windows. The Maharajah had never had much reputation for courage, and on this occasion, instead of rousing his men to action and beating off the intruders, he rushed away for safety out at the back of the palace, and round to the Residency.

Meanwhile, the first note of alarm was brought to my husband by the bearer, who woke him up at two in the morning with the report that a fight was taking place in the palace, which report was fully confirmed by the whiz of bullets over the house; and in a few minutes the Maharajah and his three brothers arrived in hot haste from the palace, trembling for their safety. Some Sepoys came with them, and a great many followers armed with swords and any sort of weapon they had managed to snatch up in the general mêlée.

My husband went out as he was, to receive the Maharajah, and got him to go into the durbar room and lie down, as he was in such a terrible state of alarm. But he refused any comfort, though he was told that he need have no fear, as even then the Ghoorkas were marching in from Langthabal, and as many as were needed could be got down from Kohima in four or five days to retake the palace which the rebel princes had got possession of. But all to no purpose.

Meanwhile my husband went away to dress, and in a very short time the detachment of the 44th had arrived from the cantonments to garrison the Residency in case of attack. But the fight was a very feeble one, owing to the immediate retreat of the Maharajah and his party, and after the first few shots all was quiet. My husband brought every argument to bear upon the Rajah to induce him to brave the matter out, and allow some efforts to be made to regain his throne; but he would not listen to any reason, and after some hours spent in fear and terror as to what the next move might be, he signified his intention to my husband of making a formal abdication of his throne for the purpose of devoting the remaining years of his life to performing a pilgrimage to the sacred city of Brinhaband, on the Ganges. He was in the Residency from two o'clock in the morning of one day to the evening of the day following, as my husband was anxious to get him to reconsider his hasty resolve to abandon his throne; but fear of the Senaputti overcame all other sensations: he persisted in putting his intentions in writing; the letter was sent informing his rebel brothers of his decision, and in the evening he left the place with a strong escort of Ghoorkas to see him safely down to Cachar.

During the hours that he spent at the Residency, an incident occurred which he (the then Maharajah) has since tried to bring up before the public as an accusation against my husband; but the real facts of the case were as follows: I have mentioned that on leaving the palace that night the Maharajah was escorted by a number of Manipuri Sepoys, all armed with rifles, besides the rag-tag and bob-tail who carried swords, and dâos, and such weapons. To avoid confusion and any unnecessary cause for alarm, the officer in charge of our escort, and my husband, considered it wiser to deprive the Manipuri Sepoys of their rifles for the time being. They were therefore all collected and stowed away in a corner of the veranda, and it was intended that they should, of course, be eventually returned to their several owners; or if further hostilities were commenced by the occupants of the palace, making it necessary to defend the Residency, each Manipuri should receive back his rifle at once, and be considered as part of our own force. But as the firing had ceased entirely in the palace, it would have been unwise to leave the Manipuri Sepoys in possession of their rifles, for they were under no sort of control, and were ready to fire without any provocation at all, a proceeding which would probably have been attended with disastrous results, as the Senaputti would not have hesitated to return the fire from his strong position in the palace, and things would have assumed a serious attitude. The Maharajah was consulted, and agreed to the proposition, and his men were disarmed for the nonce. This has since been turned into a very different tale by the exiled monarch to serve his own ends, and he has accused my husband of disarming his troops without his consent, thus disabling them from making any attempt to regain the position he had forfeited himself through abject cowardice.

At length, after nearly thirty-six hours in the Residency, during which the Maharajah would eat nothing, he made a formal abdication in writing of his throne in favour of his next brother, the Jubraj; and my husband, finding every argument of no avail, began to make the necessary arrangements for his highness's departure, which took place in the evening of the second day. Some of the ministers came to the Residency to bid him farewell, and seemed sorry that he was going; and there were some very affecting partings.

No regret seems to have been felt, however, on the Pucca Senna's departure, as he and his two younger brothers accompanied the Maharajah into his voluntary exile. The Pucca Senna had never been a favourite. He was very bad-tempered and jealous, and ready to find fault with everything, and make mischief all round. People liked the Maharajah himself, but his favourite brother was cordially disliked; and afterwards, when we were out in the district in the winter, we used to hear the opinion of the country people, and it was always that they considered it a pity the Maharajah had gone, but they did not want the Pucca Senna back.

My husband bade them farewell on the banks of the river separating the Cachar road from the Residency, and saw them safely on their way, escorted by our Ghoorkas, and then returned to begin a new régime, which was destined to last but a few months, and end so unhappily.

Meanwhile, during the attack on the palace, and victory of the rebel princes, the Jubraj had betaken himself to a place seventeen miles from Manipur, called Bishenpur, there to remain a neutral observer of the contest for the Ghuddi.* Had the Maharajah held his own, and driven the rebels out of the place as he should have done, the Jubraj would still have been on the right side by saying that he was away, and consequently did not know what was taking place in the city. As it was, he returned to Manipur as soon as matters had settled themselves in favour of the Senaputti and his adherent brothers, and accepted with calm equanimity the government of the state, and the title of regent.

There has been some confusion over the different titles given to the various members of the royal family at Manipur; and to avoid any further mistakes as to the identity of each, I cannot do better than end this chapter with a

* Ghuddi—throne.

tree showing the several princes and their denominations both before and after the flight of the Maharajah, known as Soor Chandra Singh—thus:

2. Jubraj, Heir-Apparent.	1. Soor Chandra Singh, Maharajah.	7. Pucca Senna, Commander of the horse.
3. Senaputti, Commander-in-Chief.	5. Angao Senna, Officer in charge of Tamum Road.	8. Zillah Singh, A.D.C. to the Maharajah.
4. Samoo Hengeba, Chief officer in charge of the elephants.	6. Dooloroi Hengeba, Officer in charge of doolies.	

When the Maharajah went away, he took with him, as I have said before, the three princes known as Pucca Senna, Samoo Hengeba, and Dooloroi Hengeba, leaving behind him the remaining four, who took upon themselves new titles as follows:

The Jubraj became . . Regent.
The Senaputti became . Jubraj.

Prince Angao became	.	Senaputti.
Zillah Singh ,,	.	Samoo Hengeba.

Therefore in future I shall use these titles in writing of the new Government to avoid confusion.

CHAPTER XII.

EARLY in November I returned from the hills, and went back to Manipur. Everything seemed changed by the alteration in the government of the state. There was little doubt that the new Jubraj was practically ruler of the roost, and the improvement was very great in everything. Roads that had been almost impassable in the ex-Maharajah's reign were repaired and made good enough to drive on. Bridges that had been sadly needed were erected; some of them on first-class plans, which were calculated to last three times as long as the flimsy structures which existed previously. The people seemed happier and more contented, and my husband found it much easier to work with the Manipur durbar than he had done when there were eight opinions to be consulted instead of four. There were no more petty jealousies and quarrels among the princes, and I had no fears about asking them all at once to any festivity.

At Christmas they all came to a magic-lantern performance. My husband had got one out from England, and he made the slides himself from photographs, chosing as subjects groups of Manipuris, or photographs of the princes and bits of the country. A picture of Miss Maïpâkbi was greeted with much applause on the part of the Jubraj, who, by the way, had decided to add this young lady to his other nine wives. The performance concluded with a large representation of the ex-Maharajah in royal dress. Dead silence greeted it, and an awkward pause; but my husband changed the slide almost directly to one of a humorous character, which caused everyone much amusement.

I mentioned the royal dress in the Maharajah's photograph. This was worn only on very great occasions, usually of a sacred nature. It consisted of a coat and Dhotee made of silk, of a grayish shade, embroidered all over in purple silk in a fleur-de-lis pattern. No one but a prince could wear this particular stuff; and if anyone was found with it on, whether in his house or on the public thoroughfare, he was immediately seized, and deprived of the garments in question, and everything else he happened to have on at the same time.

On one occasion the bandmaster expressed a wish to have his photograph taken, and my husband arranged to do it for him on a certain day. He arrived with a large bundle, saying that he wished to be allowed to change his attire in our grounds, as he desired to be taken in the royal dress, and could not walk from his house to ours without being subjected to the ignominious treatment I have already described. So he retreated to the largest tree he could find and retired behind it, where he hastily attired himself in the coveted robes, adding as extra adornment a cap of green satin embroidered in gold, shaped like a small tea-cosy, and curious sorts of pads, also of green satin, on the backs of his hands. He put a large red flower in his buttonhole, and borrowed my husband's watch and chain, as he had none of his own. He looked a very queer character indeed, but the photograph turned out a great success and filled him with delight, which increased tenfold when I painted one for him. He divested himself, after the picture was done, of his fine feathers, and took them away in the same dirty, unsuspicious-looking bundle in which they had arrived.

I was sorry to find that this bandmaster had left Manipur when I returned there. He had gone down to Calcutta with the ex-Maharajah, with whom he had always been a great favourite, and left the band to the tender mercies of a havildar, who knew nothing of music.

Early in January of this year, 1891, we went to Kohima to meet the chief commissioner, Mr. Quinton, and spent a very pleasant four days there. It was always such a treat to see people. Life in the station at Manipur was so dreadfully monotonous, but I had been better off than my husband, who had not seen any white faces for several months. Not that that troubled him very much. He always adapted himself to whatever were his circumstances, and made the best of them, never thinking of, and worrying himself for, the many things he had not got. But when the opportunity of getting anyone down to stay with us did arise, he was very keen about it, and while at Kohima we tried very hard to persuade the chief and his daughter to come to Manipur;

but it could not be managed, as Mr. Quinton had then arranged his tour, and had not sufficient time to spare to enable him to come such a long distance out of his way. That journey was always the difficulty, and had it not been such a lengthy one, people at Kohima would often have come down to see us at Manipur. But as a rule the whole of their leave was swamped in coming and going.

From Kohima we went to Tummu, in Burmah, returning first to the Residency for a few days. This was my first visit to Burmah. My husband had gone down the year before, but I had been too ill to accompany him, and had stayed behind. We had lovely weather, and enjoyed the journey there immensely. The scenery on the way is lovely, and as the forests are not so dense as those on the Cachar road, one can get magnificent views of the surrounding country every now and then. Range after range of mountains rise gloriously around you, as you wend your way among the leafy glades and shimmering forests which clothe their rugged sides. Cool and green near you, growing purple as you leave them behind, and becoming faintly blue as they outline themselves on the far horizon, these mountains fill you with admiration. Forests of teak rise on each side of you as you get nearer Tummu, and the heat becomes much greater.

After five days we arrived at our camp, which was situated on the boundary between Manipur and Burmah, at a place called Mori Thana. Here we stayed, living in a pagoda, in company with several figures of Buddha and many other minor deities, indicating that the building was sacred. The Burmese are very fond of flowers, and they always place vases of gaily-coloured blossoms in front of their gods, and small punkahs to keep them cool. The pagoda we were lodged in was built, like all Burmese houses, on piles, about three feet from the ground. The climate is so damp that they are obliged to be raised, or the floor of the house would very soon become rotten. Everything at Tummu was quite different to Manipur: the women dressed in much gayer colours, and did their hair more picturesquely in large knobs on the top of their heads, into which they stuck tiny fans, or flowers, or brightly-coloured beads. All the women smoke, even the young ones, and one seldom sees them without a cigar in their mouths. These cigars are made of very mild tobacco, grown in their own gardens, and dried by themselves. They roll a quantity up tight in the dried leaf of the Indian corn-plant, and tie the ends round with fine silk. They are longer and fatter than those smoked in England, and the Burmese girls at Tummu did not approve at all of some from Belat which my husband gave them, as they were too strong for them.

The Myouk* came out to see us the day after we arrived. He was a Burman, of course, but spoke English very well indeed, and was most anxious to be of use to us. He was dressed in silk of the most delicate shade of pink, with a yellow turban, and he rode in on a charming bay pony, looking altogether very picturesque. We informed him that we intended riding into Tummu, so he politely offered to escort us and show us the way; and he rode back with us, and we found him a very pleasant companion. I was delighted with Tummu, and we wandered about in the village, looking at the pagodas, and in-

* Myouk — a civil officer in Burmah corresponding to an extra assistant commissioner in other parts of India.

vesting in the curiosities to be got in the place. We bought some lovely pieces of silk, and some quaintly-carved wooden chessmen. The Burmese have a game of chess almost identical with ours —the same number of pieces, and a board marked out in black and white squares. The rules of the game, too, are almost exactly the same, but the pieces are named differently, and carved to represent elephants and pagodas, instead of castles and knights. The Manipuris also played chess, and I once saw a lovely set of chessmen carved in ivory and gold that the Maharajah possessed. The ones I got at Tummu at the time of which I write were made of oak, and were evidently ancient, which added a charm in my eyes, though the Myouk was very anxious to get a new set made for me. However, I went on the principle of a bird in the hand being better than two in the bush, and marched away with my trophies on the spot. We were returning to our camp for breakfast, when the Myouk informed us that there was another Sahib living in the place, a military Sahib of the name of Grant. This was news indeed to us, as we had had no idea when at Manipur that we had any neighbours nearer than Kohima, ninety-six miles away from us, and here was someone only sixty-five—quite a short journey.

My husband said he would go and look the "military Sahib'" up, but before he could do so the Sahib in question had looked us up. I do not think Mr. Grant, as he then was, ever expected to have a lady sprung on him unawares, and he seemed a little bothered over his clothes, which were those generally assumed by bachelors when they are safe from any possibility of female intrusion in the solitude of a jungle outpost. However, he soon remedied that. He went away to his bungalow after I had made him promise that he would come back later; and when he did return it was in attire worthy of better things than a camp dinner with camp discomforts. But he was so bright and jolly that he cheered us both up, and made all the difference during our four days at Tummu. We went to tea with him in his tiny quarters, and had great jokes over the "army ration"—sugar and butter—and the other etceteras of a temporary encampment. He was quartered at Tummu in charge of a part of his regiment, and considering the loneliness of his surroundings and the distance he was away from any sort of civilization, we marvelled that he was so cheery and full of spirits.

One day he came out to our camp at Mori Thana and helped me to make a cake, which turned out afterwards, I am bound honestly to say, burnt to a cinder. My husband made some cutting allusions to it, and told me that it would save our having to invest in charcoal for some days to come, and added many other remarks of the same kind; but, nothing daunted, Mr. Grant and I set to work and carved up that cake, discovering as a reward a certain amount in the middle which was quite eatable and altogether excellent, which my husband also condescended to try after some persuasion, and pronounced fair.

We were all very keen about orchids, and these grew abundantly on the trees round about Tummu, so we went for long rambles, and returned always with armfuls of them.

We were very sorry to bid good-bye to Mr. Grant at the end of our stay in Burmah, and we tried to persuade him to get leave and come up to us for a time for some duck-shooting on the Logtak Lake.

On the way back we got the news that we were to have two visitors, Mr. Melville, the superintendent of the telegraph department, in Assam; and Lieutenant Simpson, of the 43rd Ghoorka Rifles, who had been ordered down to Manipur from Kohima to inspect some military stores which had been left behind at the Langthabal cantonment, when the troops went away. We were very pleased at hearing they were coming, as even the ordinary two or three visitors who had come every winter on duty in previous years had failed us. Mr. Melville arrived about ten days after we returned to Manipur from Tummu, but Mr. Simpson came almost at once. I had known him well in Shillong, and we had always been great friends. He was very clever, and a wonderful musician, and nothing pleased him better than to be allowed to play the piano for hours, whatever he liked, without interruption. My husband and he soon became good friends. Their tastes were congenial, and Mr. Simpson was always delighted to shoot with him, and he got on very well with the princes, especially the

Jubraj, who liked looking at his guns and talking military "shop" with him. Several shooting-parties were organized by the prince, and the Shikaris always returned with good bags.

Mr. Melville stayed only three days with us, but he promised to return for another two on his way back from Tummu, where he was going to inspect his office. On Sunday, February 21 (the day Mr. Simpson arrived), in the evening we were surprised by getting a telegram from the Chief Commissioner, the gist of which was as follows:

"I propose to visit Manipur shortly. Have roads and rest-houses put in order. Further directions and dates to follow."

We were electrified! Why was the chief coming like this suddenly? The telegram gave no details, and the one and only cause for his unexpected visit that we could think of was that it had something to do with the ex-Maharajah. This individual had been, during these months, in Calcutta, from which place he had concocted and despatched more than one letter to Government, begging for a reconsideration of his case, and help to regain the kingdom which he had been unjustly deprived of by the Jubraj, assisted by my husband's influence.

Curiosity had naturally been rife at Manipur as to whether the exiled monarch would be restored by our Government, and the Jubraj and Tongal General had never ceased asking my husband his opinion about it. We knew full well that if such a step were contemplated, the fulfilment of it would be a difficult operation, as we were aware of the bitter feeling which existed against the ex-Maharajah, and more especially against his brother, the Pucca Senna. From private sources we had heard that arms, ammunition, and food were being collected by order of the Jubraj inside the palace.

This information came to me quite casually one day. We used to employ a Manipuri Shikari* to shoot wild duck for us during the cold weather, when my husband was not able to get them himself, and I sent for this man one day, and told him what I wanted him to get for us. He said

* Shikari—sportsman, or a man who will go out shooting for you or with you.

he was not able to shoot, as the Jubraj had ordered him, as well as all the other men in his village, to bring their guns into the palace arsenal, and that all the villages in the neighbourhood had received similar commands. I let the man go, and went and repeated the story to my husband, who remarked that it looked as though preparations were being made to resist the ex-Maharajah, should he return to Manipur. Of course, on the receipt of the telegram from the Chief Commissioner, my husband had to inform the durbar of his approaching visit. Curiosity reached an overwhelming pitch, and the efforts of the Jubraj and his colleagues to find out what was going to happen were unceasing. They never quite believed that my husband was as ignorant as they were themselves about things, and invariably went away much disturbed. We ourselves were just as curious and longing to know what was really coming to pass.

In the meanwhile I had arranged to leave for England.

For more than three years our one talk had been of furlough and home, and now that the date of sailing had been really fixed, it seemed almost impossible to put it off in order to be at Manipur waiting to see the results of the Chief's visit. My husband said, however, that he thought it would be more prudent if I arranged to go by an earlier steamer, to be out of danger in the event of anything serious happening, and consequently all the necessary arrangements were made for my departure. I couldn't help feeling that I would rather stay, however, and, as I said to a friend in writing home, "see the fun," and my packing did not progress satisfactorily at all.

Mr. Simpson was very keen to remain at Manipur, too; but all his work was done there, and there was really no reason for his stopping. He wired to the colonel of his regiment for permission to remain, and my husband backed the request up, so eventually the necessary leave was granted, and he was delighted at the mere idea of a disturbance which might mean fighting. Of course the sudden alteration in my plans did not escape the notice of the Jubraj, and in fact the durbar itself. It seemed as though the whole State was on the *qui vive*, to discover any slight clue to the mystery which surrounded the visit of the Chief Commissioner. My sudden determination to depart was looked upon as possessing a very serious meaning indeed. I was flying from danger. This was the prevailing idea, and the Tongal General asked me point blank one day whether it was the case or not, at the same time begging me to put off going till after the Chief had left Manipur. The princes used every persuasion they could to induce me to remain, and they and the old general came more than once with messages from the Maharajah to the same effect. We explained to them that my passage was taken and paid for in the steamer, and that the money would be forfeited if I failed to sail on a certain date; but this had no weight, and they did not seem to like my going away at all, and begged me to stay on. These persuasions, added to my husband's extreme reluctance to let me go, and my own wish to remain, carried the day.

About ten days before Mr. Quinton arrived we heard for certain that the object of his visit was *not* the restoration of the ex-Maharajah, and so, after much coaxing from me, my husband, thinking of course that no danger could now be possible, allowed me to stay. I remember so well how lightly we talked over coming events, and my husband saying that if anything did happen, they would make me a nice safe place in one of the cellars under the house. Could we but foresee what is behind the dark veil with which the future is enveloped, and know that sometimes in our idlest moments we are standing as it were on the brink of a grave, is there one of us who would not rather die at once than struggle on into the abyss of desolation and death awaiting us in the near future? And yet it is undoubtedly a merciful Providence that orders our comings and goings from day to day in such a manner that we cannot peer into the mist of approaching years, and discover for ourselves what fate awaits each one of us. "Sufficient unto the day is the evil thereof."

CHAPTER XIII.

Of course there were a great many preparations to be made in honour of the Chief Commissioner's visit. The question which occupied my attention most was how to feed so many. The resources of the country in the way of food were very limited. Beef was an impossibility, as no one was allowed to kill a cow, and mutton was almost equally unprocurable. The Jubraj kept a few sheep for their wool, and once in a way he killed one or two of them to provide a dinner for all the Mussulman officers and servants in the palace; but this occurred very seldom. We lived on ducks and fowls all the year round, and managed fairly well; but having to provide for sixteen people was a different matter altogether. My husband made several valiant attempts to secure some sheep from Cachar, and after much difficulty he got four, and we heard they had commenced their march up to Manipur. But they never arrived alive. The drover was a most conscientious person, and took the trouble to bring the four dead carcases up to the Residency for our inspection, to assure us that the poor animals had died natural deaths, which we thought very touching on his part.

We were in despair over our commissariat, but at last that invaluable domestic, the bearer, came to the rescue, and proposed that as we could not get genuine mutton, we should invest in a goat. One often eats goat in India, deluding one's self with the idea that it is sheep, because it has cost one as dear, and the native butcher swears that he is giving one the best mutton in the district. But after you have kept house for a year or two, and got to know the wily Oriental, you are able to distinguish truly the sheep from the goats. Be that as it may, when one can't get one thing, one must content one's self with the best substitute; and on this occasion I was very grateful to the bearer for his timely suggestion, and commissioned him to search the neighbourhood for the desired goat, which after some days was discovered, and brought to the Residency for inspection. We had a committee of four on it, and came to the conclusion that it was a most estimable animal, and altogether worthy of providing dinner for a Chief Commissioner. So we bought that goat, tethered him in the kitchen-garden, and fed him every day and all day. He grew enormous, and slept a great deal when he was not eating, which was his favourite occupation.

Meanwhile the days went by, and at last only one week remained before the Chief's arrival, and by that time we knew that he was bringing an escort of four hundred men with him and several officers; but we did not know how long they were going to stay, or why so many were coming, or whether they were going on to Burmah. A telegram had come some days previously, telling my husband to get coolies ready to take the party to Tummu, and he thought from that that it was Mr. Quinton's intention to pay a visit to that part of the valley; but everything seemed uncertain, and the Manipuris were very curious to find out what it all meant.

About a week before the Chief arrived Mr. Gurdon was sent on to see my husband, and talk over matters with him; but even then we were ignorant of what was really intended, and it was only on the day before they all arrived—Saturday, March 21—that my husband was told all by Mr. Quinton himself, whom he had ridden out ten miles to meet. He started out in the morning for Sengmai, the first halting-stage on the road to Kohima from Manipur, and on his arrival he wired to me, telling me to expect eleven to breakfast the next day, which, with ourselves, Mr. Melville, and Mr. Simpson made fifteen.

Mr. Simpson and I went for a ride that evening, and as we were returning we both remarked the great number of Manipuri Sepoys we met, hurrying into the citadel. They swarmed along the road, and on getting near the big gate of the palace we had some difficulty in getting our horses through the crowds which were streaming into the fort, and I was quite glad when we got back safely into the Residency grounds again. My husband returned about seven from Sengmai, very tired and very much worried at all he had heard. I went into his little private office with him, and there he told me of what was to take place on the morrow, making me promise not to breathe a word of it to either Mr. Melville or Mr. Simpson, as it was to be kept a dead secret. He wrote off at once to the regent, telling him that the Chief Commissioner would hold a durbar on the following day at twelve, at which he hoped all the princes would appear, and then we went away and had dinner. It was difficult to talk of other things while our minds were full of the information my husband had received, and I was very glad when the evening ended, and our two visitors had gone to bed.

It had been decided to recognise the regent as Maharajah, but his brother, the Jubraj, was to be arrested at the durbar the next day, taken out of the country, and banished for several years. That was the news my husband brought. It has been hinted of late by some that the friendship which we had both entertained for the Jubraj was *infra dig.*, and contrary to the usual mode of procedure adopted by Anglo-Indian officials in their intercourse with the rulers of native states. But when first we went to Manipur, my husband was told that he must endeavour to establish friendly feelings between the princes and himself, and that he was to make a point of becoming acquainted with their language, in order to acquire an influence for good over each member of the Maharajah's family and over the state itself.

I do not think there was ever any loss of dignity or unbecoming familiarity in my husband's friendship for the Jubraj. Full well that prince, and all the other members of the durbar, knew that where things went wrong they would not escape his notice and reproof, even as when they went right he would give praise where praise was due; and if such a friendship were distasteful and unusual in similar circumstances, why was it never commented on by those in whose power it was to approve or disapprove, and who knew that it existed? Small wonder was it that we were both very sorry to hear of the fate which was in store for the Jubraj. We remembered all the little acts of courtesy and kindness which he had performed to help make our lonely existence brighter, isolated as we were from any English friends, and we knew how much he would feel being sent out of Manipur at so short a notice. However, we could do nothing by talking it over, and so went to rest ourselves, resolving to think no more about it until the next day.

The morning of the 22nd broke clear and beautiful over the valley. The place had never looked more lovely. Clusters of yellow roses blossomed on the walls of the house, and the scent of the heliotrope greeted me as I went into the veranda to watch my husband start to meet Mr. Quinton. There was a delightful sense of activity about the place, and one felt that something of more than ordinary importance was about to take place; white tents peeped out from amongst the trees surrounding the house, and the camp prepared for the Sepoys stretched along under our wall at the end of the lake. Mr. Simpson and I strolled down the drive, out into the road, to see the preparations in honour of Mr. Quinton's coming. Chairs were placed near the principal palace gate, and a carpet, and a table with flowers on it; and there were a great many Manipuri Sepoys lining the road by which he was expected to arrive.

I was called back to the house by the bearer with a piece of intelligence which almost took my breath away—*the goat was dying!* I raced back to the Residency, and rushed to the scene of action. There on the ground lay the goat, breathing his last, and with his departing spirit went all my dreams of legs of mutton, chops and cutlets. I sent to the house for bottles of hot beer and quarts of brandy, and I poured gallons of liquid down the creature's throat; but all to no purpose, and after giving one last heartrending groan, he expired at my feet. I could have wept. The pains that had been taken with that goat to make it fat and well-favoured for the delectation of my friends! and then that it should shuffle off this mortal coil on the very day fixed for its execution was altogether heartrending. I think I really should have found relief in tears, had not my attention been aroused by the sound of the salute being fired from the palace, which meant that the Chief and his party had appeared in sight. So I turned away sadly, after giving orders to have the creature buried, and proceeded to the house, where I met Mr. Simpson and Mr. Melville. They both expressed much sympathy, but we could not help seeing the funny side of the affair, and ended by laughing very heartily over the sad end to my mutton scheme.

Twelve times did the gun boom from the palace, and by the time the twelfth had sounded,

Mr. Quinton, accompanied by Colonel Skene and my husband, had arrived at the house, followed shortly by the other officers, who had remained at the camp to see their men comfortably housed and settled. We all went in to breakfast, but I noticed that my husband seemed troubled about something, as he scarcely spoke at all, and I wondered what fresh news he had heard. However, I had no opportunity of speaking to him at all, and the conversation flowed merrily round the table. I knew very few of the Chief Commissioner's party, as all the officers belonging to the 42nd Ghoorka Rifles were total strangers to me. Of the rest, Mr. Brackenbury and I were perhaps the oldest friends. He had been stationed at Manipur before, when he first came to the place, and we had seen a great deal of him, so were glad that he had come on this occasion.

As soon as breakfast was over, preparations were made for the durbar, and the work of the day began. I had no opportunity of speaking to my husband until he was dressing for the ceremony, and then I went and asked him what was bothering him; and he told me that *he* had been ordered to arrest the Jubraj at the close of the durbar. It is not for me to give an opinion on this point at all, and whether such a course of action was honourable or not; but it was only natural that my husband should feel sorry that he had been chosen to carry out such a proceeding. To be obliged to arrest a man himself with whom he had been on friendly terms for nearly three years, and see him treated like a common felon, without being able to defend himself, was naturally a hard task, and my husband felt it bitterly.

I summoned up courage to ask whether some other officer might not make the arrest, as it had to be made; but was told that the Jubraj would probably feel it less if my husband did it, as they were good friends. Precautions were taken to prevent his escaping. The doors of the durbar room were all locked with the exception of the one by which the princes would enter, and guards were stationed in the adjoining rooms, as well as all round the house and in the verandas. Most of the officers were ignorant of what was intended, and they were joking with me, and trying to find out whether I were in the secret or not, while we were waiting for the Maharajah to arrive.

Meanwhile the written orders of the Government of India had to be translated into Manipuri, and for this purpose two of the office clerks and the Burmese interpreter were brought to the Residency and given the papers to translate. The orders were lengthy, and the translation of them took some time. Each of the clerks had a sentry placed over him, and they all had to swear an oath that they would not divulge one word to anyone of the contents of the papers given them to translate. Some time before they were completed the regent and *all* his brothers arrived at the Residency gate. I have laid particular stress on the word *all,* because it has been said that the Jubraj did not accompany his brother on this occasion, though subsequent evidence has since appeared showing that he was really present with the rest. Had there been no reason for keeping the princes waiting at the gate, things might have ended very differently. But that delay enabled some of the Manipuri Sepoys to gain admission into the Residency grounds, from where they could take note of all the proceedings. They made good use of their opportunities, marked the distribution of our forces, saw the Ghoorkas lining the entrance-steps, and the officers in uniform in attendance outside. Some of them even strolled round to the back of the house, and there they saw the same preparations—Sepoys on the steps, and guards about the grounds.

Of course the Manipuris did not keep this to themselves, but made their way out again to the Jubraj, and told him of all they had seen; and he took the opportunity to return to his house with his brother, the Senaputti, giving out as an excuse that he felt too ill to remain waiting about in the hot sun. He had not been well for some time before, but whether he really felt as indisposed on this occasion as he affirmed is open to doubt. He had already made the acquaintance of the Chief Commissioner, and so had the Senaputti, as the latter had ridden out to Sengmai on the Saturday to meet Mr. Quinton, and the Jubraj had also met him seven miles out of Manipur on Sunday morning.

When, therefore, the regent was asked to come on to the Residency, he came, accompanied by his youngest brother only, Prince Zillah

Singh, the Tongal General, and some other less important ministers. As soon as my husband saw that his highness had arrived without the two elder brothers, he informed Mr. Quinton, who sent out word to the regent that the durbar could not be held without the attendance of the Jubraj and Senaputti. My husband had a long conversation with the regent before his highness came into the house, and the latter agreed to send for his brothers to the palace, coming himself into the Residency to await their arrival. It seemed a long time before the messenger returned from the palace. The old Tongal was so seedy at the time that we wondered at his having been able to put in an appearance at all. I went into the drawing-room, and found the old man asleep on the floor, and got him to lie down on a sofa with a pillow under his head, where he very soon slumbered peacefully. At last the regent's messenger returned with the reply from the Jubraj that he was too ill to leave his house, and hoped Mr. Quinton would excuse his appearing; so the durbar was postponed till the next morning, Monday, March 23, at eight o'clock, and it was impressed upon his highness that his two brothers *must* attend. They then went away. There is little doubt that, from this moment, some inkling of what was intended penetrated the minds of the princes and their ministers, just as all the officers guessed that it was the Jubraj who was "wanted."

However, business being over for that day, we set to work to amuse ourselves as best we could, strolling about the grounds, and into the bazaar in the evening. We had already arranged to have a polo-match one day during Mr. Quinton's visit, in which the princes were to play; and the regent had promised to have a review of his troops, which was always a pretty sight. In addition to this, the band had been lent to us to play every evening at dinner; and we were to have a Manipuri nautch on the Monday, followed by a Naga dance the next evening, if the weather permitted. This programme had been drawn up by my husband and myself two or three weeks before Mr. Quinton's arrival, but it has since come to light that the Jubraj suspected us of treachery in asking him to arrange and be present at these nautches.

We had never seen so many people in the

Residency at once as there were that Sunday night at dinner—fifteen in all. I felt rather forlorn, being the only lady present, and wished that I had even one familiar spirit in the shape of another woman to keep me company.

The band was very much appreciated, and everything seemed very bright and cheery. No thought of evil troubled any of us, for little we knew that it was the last evening we were to spend in peace there all together.

The next day Mr. Melville was to leave us. I had tried to persuade him to stay longer, as he had only been two days with us before, and had seen nothing of the place; but his time was precious, and he had his work to do in a great many other places, so we could not get him to alter his arrangements. He agreed to compromise matters by remaining until the afternoon of the following day, the 23rd, and about eleven the party broke up and retired to rest.

CHAPTER XIV.

It is now some time since the events took place which I am recording here, and not one vestige of the past remains to help me in my work, not a single scrap of writing or note of any kind; yet the smallest detail of those few terrible days is engraved so indelibly upon my memory that it seems but the occurrence of yesterday, and I need no reference to help me in my description of a catastrophe which almost outrivals some of the horrors of the Mutiny.

We were all up early on the morning of the 23rd. The durbar was fixed to take place at eight, and the rooms had to be prepared for the ceremony. But when eight o'clock came, it brought only a message from the palace, saying that the Jubraj was too ill to leave his house, and therefore the regent had not come; so the red cloth arranged for his reception was put away, and a consultation took place between the

Chief and my husband as to what the next move should be.

It was decided to make one last attempt to get the princes to attend, and then if that failed, other measures were to be resorted to. But twelve o'clock brought no better results, and about four my husband was sent to the palace to see the Jubraj, and convey to him personally the orders of the Government, and use all his influence to persuade the prince to give himself up quietly, telling him at the same time that the proposed banishment was not to last for ever, but that it would depend chiefly on his good behaviour, and eventually, at the death of his brother, the regent, he (the Jubraj) would be allowed to return to Manipur, and ascend the throne as Maharajah. It was a veritable hornets' nest into which my husband ventured that afternoon, accompanied only by his friend Mr. Simpson. He would not take even a single orderly with him, knowing in what an excited state the whole palace was at that time. It was crowded with Sepoys, collected, the regent told him, for the review which we had desired to witness. I got very anxious about them both when more than an hour had passed and they had not returned, but when my husband did come back I knew at a glance that his mission had failed. He said the Jubraj was certainly very unwell. He had had some difficulty at first in persuading the prince to come and see him at all, but after finding out from his people that the two Sahibs had come quite alone, the Jubraj had himself carried down to see them in a litter. The exertion caused him to faint, and my husband said that there was no doubt as to his illness, and that he found him in high fever.

Shortly before this visit to the palace took place, Mr. Melville started off on the first stage of his journey to Kohima. He intended travelling as far as Sengmai that day, a distance of ten miles. My husband tried to make him reconsider his decision to go, and I added my persuasions to his. We did not like the look of things at all, and how matters would end was, to say the least, very uncertain.

I remember so well our all standing on the steps of the Residency that afternoon, watching the coolies collecting Mr. Melville's luggage, and begging him to remain even one day longer with us, for fear of anything going wrong; and I remember equally well his answer: "Thank you very much, Mrs. Grimwood," he said, "but do not fear for me. I am not important enough to be captured by these Manipuris. I shall get on all right, never fear;" and in a few more minutes he had left us. But the thoughts of his going away like that, alone, without any guard to protect him, troubled me more than once that afternoon, and I could not get it out of my head. Matters assumed a serious aspect indeed when my husband returned about six o'clock from the palace with the news that he had been unsuccessful with regard to the Jubraj. There was only one way, then, out of the difficulty, and that was to place the affair in the hands of the military, and apply force where persuasion had failed. It was a council of war, indeed, and everything seemed to combine to fill me with sensations of dread for what was going to happen. I could not feel the excitement that took possession of the men when the chances of a probable fight became known. Such an idea filled me with alarm and horror. The place had a deserted look about it, and on the principal road, as a rule crowded with people at that hour, not a soul was visible.

The clouds had been gathering up all the afternoon, and about seven o'clock a terrific thunderstorm occurred, and darkness set in, which was only lit up now and then by brilliant flashes of lightning. I busied myself about the house, where I found a state of confusion reigning. A number of the servants had taken French leave and departed, scenting danger.

My old ayah was among the first to go. She had been with me four years, and had followed me about faithfully till now; but at the first sign of danger she packed up her belongings and went off. I wondered where she had taken refuge, for she had a good many enemies, and was not a native of Manipur, so had no home or relations in the place to whom she could fly for protection. I felt her desertion very much. She was only a native, but she was at any rate a woman, and better than no one in a case like that. However, there was no good to be got out of thinking over her departure, and I had as much as I could do as it was to keep the other servants up to the mark, and get them to understand that dinner that evening would have to be gone through the same as usual. Mr. Quinton and three of the others amused themselves by playing whist until dinner time, as, of course, going out was an impossibility; and I went to the kitchen to superintend the arrangements there, and to make preparations for the next day, as I knew that if there were fighting going on, I should be left without a single servant, and so resolved to get as much work out of them while they were there as was possible. We made a quantity of soup that night, as I thought it would be useful, and cooked some fowls to provide us with something to eat the next day in case of accidents. And then we had dinner.

No one seemed inclined to speak much that evening. With me conversation was almost an impossibility, and the rest were too excited about the morrow to be able to talk and laugh as they had done the day before. It was a relief to me when dinner was over. I felt nervous and low-spirited, and very lonely, quite out of place amongst those men whose profession it was to fight, and who were longing for the next morning.

Thoughts of England and of all whom I loved there, flocked through my mind, and I wondered what they would say if they could see us then, and know the possible danger that threatened us and our home. My husband was troubled at the thoughts of my being in the place at such a time, and he blamed himself for having agreed to my staying, though I had done so of my own free will. Even then we did not dream of any really serious ending. We expected that the Jubraj would fight well—in fact, the officers and Sepoys were hoping that the resistance would be strong, and my husband was afraid that the house might get knocked about, and some of our property destroyed; but serious alarm for our own safety never entered our heads. This was the night of the 23rd, the date that we had originally fixed for the Manipuri nautch to take place; but under the circumstances we did not think it likely that the girls would come. Mr. Brackenbury amused us by singing comic songs, accompanying himself on his banjo after dinner, and all went to bed early, as everyone had to be up at three the next morning.

It was a lovely moonlight night, and my husband and I walked up and down in the garden for some time after our guests had gone. I felt restless and unhappy, but he did his best to reassure me and make me believe that we should all be perfectly safe. Just before we were preparing to go in, the sentry challenged at the gate, and appeared a few minutes afterwards with a Manipuri, who had been sent from the palace to inquire whether we wished to have the nautch or not, saying at the same time, that the girls who were to dance were waiting outside in the road if we wanted them. Of course we told him it was much too late to think of such a thing at that time, and the man left the place. We believed that he had really been sent to spy out the land, and find out what preparations, if any, we had been making. If that were his mission, he must have been seriously disappointed, for the whole place, and everyone in it, was wrapt in slumber, with the exception of my husband and myself, and we very often walked about the grounds late on moonlight nights, so there was nothing unusual in our doing so on this occasion. There were a few extra sentries on guard, but chiefly at the back of the house, and the presence of the Chief

Commissioner was quite sufficient cause for a larger guard than usual.

At last we turned in too, one to sleep as unconcernedly as ever, knowing not that it was his last night upon earth; the other to lie awake, listening to the hours as they were struck out on the gong down at the quarter-guard, and wonder what the ending of the next day would bring. I never closed my eyes all through the watches of that night—the last I was destined to spend in Manipur—and when three o'clock came I woke my husband, and told him that the hour had come when we were all to get up, and the work of day commenced.

It was a bitterly cold morning, and quite dark. I dressed quickly, putting on a warm, tight-fitting winter dress. We had a sort of scratch breakfast of eggs and bread-and-butter about 3.30 a.m.; but most of the officers had theirs at the camp, and started from there, so that I did not know when they actually left to commence the attack. My husband accompanied Colonel Skene, much to my distress, as I thought he would have stayed at the Residency, being a civilian; but he seemed just as keen on going as the others, and I had to make the best of it. Mr. Quinton, Mr. Cossins, and I all went off to the telegraph-office, which was situated at the end of the drive, about three hundred yards from the Residency. It was well built and fairly strong, the basement being made of stone, and there was a similar building on the opposite side, which my husband used as an office for himself, the lower half of which contained the treasury. Here we took up our position, going up into the telegraph-office first to send a message to the Government of India, giving details of all that had occurred up to date. Mr. Cossins, who was acting as secretary to the Chief Commissioner, brought the telegram down, and while we were waiting and watching the Baboo* despatch it, we heard the first shot fired in the palace, which was followed up quickly by others, and we knew then that the fight had begun.

By this time the dawn was breaking, and streaks of daylight were dispelling the darkness around. It seemed difficult to me to realize what was really taking place. I had heard firing

* Baboo—native clerk.

in the palace so often that it seemed almost impossible to understand that a sterner game was being played now, and one which was to cost both sides so dear. Only half the telegram had been sent, when we were startled by the sudden advent of a bullet through the office window at our elbows. It crashed through the glass, breaking it to pieces, and went into the wall opposite. My heart went to my mouth with fright, and I left the place with considerable rapidity, taking up a more secure position below, where I was fairly protected by the stone basement of the building. Mr. Cossins occupied his time in taking several journeys up to the house, where he mounted to the roof to discover whether he could see what was going on inside the palace wall; but it was impossible, as the Jubraj's house, which we knew was being attacked, was some distance off, and hidden from us by intervening buildings. It was situated near the outer wall of the palace, and our men seemed to have taken a very short time in getting up to it.

The whole palace was fortified. Five walls surrounded the Maharajah's enclosure. The outer of these was much broken, and of no great height; but the inner ones were very strong, built of brick and supplied with bastions, and they surrounded the inner palace on all four sides. On three sides of the outer wall was a canal, very deep and wide. It was here that the great boat-races took place every year, and the water was always kept weeded and clean for those events. The whole citadel was built with a view of resisting attack in the time before Burmah was annexed, when armies of raiders used to come down upon Manipur with hostile intent; and it was a place which could easily be held against an attacking force, provided big guns were not brought to bear upon it. The Manipuris were well armed, and supplied with ammunition. The Maharajah had four mountain guns which had been presented to his father by our Government in return for services which he had rendered in times gone by. The Jubraj understood perfectly how to work these guns. We had seen him fire them himself for our amusement on an occasion already described, and we knew he would be perfectly cognizant of their powers of destruction when the opportunity occurred to bring them into play against us. Of course we, who were left at the Residency, did not know what was going on round the Jubraj's house, where all the firing seemed to come from. From time to time stray bullets came over our heads where we sat down at the telegraph-office. I thought it was very exciting then, and the little Ghoorkas, who had remained to keep guard over the place, were constantly running out on to the road in front of our entrance-gate, to see whether they could discover what was happening. They did not like being inactive at all.

About half-past ten my husband returned, and came to the treasury to get out some of the reserve ammunition which had been stored there. He only stayed a few minutes, talking to me before rejoining Colonel Skene. He told me that the Jubraj's house had been captured after a good fight, and that our men were in possession of it, and the principal gateway besides, and had taken a good many prisoners. I asked if anyone had been hurt, and he said there were grave rumours about Lieutenant Brackenbury. No one seemed to be certain of his whereabouts, while some affirmed that he had been wounded, and others that he had been killed. We were very anxious about him, but my husband said that it was all uncertain, and he might be perfectly safe all the time; and of course we hoped he was all right.

About twelve Mr. Quinton and I went up to the house, but long before going he had made another attempt to get the telegram to the Government of India despatched, and had found that the wires had been cut on all sides, so all hope of communication from that source was abandoned. We were rather hungry by twelve, as no one had eaten much at the hasty repast at three in the morning, and we were very glad of some hot tea and sandwiches now. I went on a voyage of discovery round the house. One or two servants still remained, but they seemed very frightened, and were saying many prayers to their gods for their safety. A stray bullet or so had hit the walls of the house, knocking off some of the plaster, but otherwise everything looked the same as usual.

We returned to the office in about an hour, after I had seen that all the preparations for lunch were made. The cook had departed, but the bearer and I between us managed to get things ready in a fashion. I took a book to read with me, and busied myself in that manner until, about one o'clock, Colonel Skene and some of his officers, with my husband, returned from the scene of action. Our first inquiries were for Mr. Brackenbury, and then it became evident that something serious had happened to him, and all our fears were aroused. After that, things seemed to assume quite a different aspect, for the officers were all talking so gravely together, and did not seem quite satisfied with the way things were going.

However, we went back to the Residency to get something to eat. All had returned with the exception of Mr. Simpson and Captain Butcher, who were still at the Jubraj's house, and Mr. Brackenbury, whose exact whereabouts were unknown. We had commenced lunch, when my husband asked me if I would give orders that some food should be sent to the two officers who were not able to leave their posts, and I went away to a little room adjoining the dining-room and commenced cutting sandwiches for them, as the servants had disappeared, and one had to get everything for one's self or go without.

I had been busily engaged for about ten minutes, when I heard a sound which filled me with alarm, and a bullet crashed through the window above my head. It frightened me more than the one at the telegraph-office had done, and I dropped my knife, left the sandwiches as they were, and rushed into the dining-room. All the officers meanwhile had gone out, and had found that the Manipuris had crept round to the back of the Residency and commenced an attack upon us, using as cover the Naga village which lay between our grounds and the river. This was a clever move on their part, and it was some time before the troops could drive them back, as most of our men were engaged in holding the posts inside the palace captured early in the morning, and this left only a small guard for the Residency, treasury offices, and Sepoys' camp. Eventually our party set fire to the Naga village, and drove the Manipuris out. Bullets had made their way through the window-panes and doors of the dining-room, and had smashed some of the breakfast-things and the glass on the sideboard. It was difficult to find out the most secure place in the house, as the firing was hot in the front of the Residency by this time, and the walls, being only lath and plaster, were little or no protection.

My husband suggested my descending to the cellars, which were under the house and built of stone; but I did not like the idea, and remembered how scornful I had been when we had talked over matters weeks before, and he had joked about the snug corner he would make ready for me in the basement of the house. So I made up my mind to remain above-board, so to speak, until the worst came to the worst. It was heart-rending to see the work of destruction which was proceeding in the different rooms meanwhile. The windows were broken, and every now and then bullets crashed into the rooms, smashing different things—first a picture, then a vase, then a photograph. All my beloved household gods seemed coming to grief under my very eyes, and I was powerless to save them. We did try to collect some of the most valuable of our belongings together and put them away in a heap in the durbar room, which at that time had escaped with only one broken pane; but it was dangerous work going into the front rooms to remove them, for as the afternoon went on the firing became hotter, and bullets rained into the house at every second.

It must have been about half-past four that the big guns began to be played against us. It had been found necessary to concentrate the whole of our force on the Residency and outbuildings, such as the treasury and offices, and this entailed abandoning all the positions captured in the early part of the day inside the outer wall of the palace, and bringing all the men together. The wounded had to be recovered from all directions and conveyed to the hospital, which was some distance from the Residency.

Lieutenant Brackenbury had been discovered lying on the bank of the river which flowed north of the palace, where he had fallen shortly after the attack was made early in the morning. He had mistaken the direction, having got the wrong side of the wall near the Jubraj's house, from which point he had been exposed to a heavy fire from the enemy. It was only a marvel that he was still alive when eventually discovered, for he had remained where he fell the whole of that day, and the Manipuris had never ceased firing at him as he lay. When his exact whereabouts did become known, it was a difficult and dangerous task to remove him. Efforts had been made by some of the Sepoys to drag him away, and a native officer had been mortally wounded in the attempt. At last, about four o'clock in the afternoon, he was rescued and brought into the hospital, and it was found that he had received terrible injuries, being wounded in several places.

The sound of the first shell which whizzed over the Residency made me speechless with terror. I had heard the boom of the guns in the morning, and knew that they had been used to try and drive Captain Butcher's party out of the Jubraj's house, which had been captured; but they had sounded some distance off, and I had not realized how terrible they could be until they were turned against our own house.

The cellars were by this time unavoidable. My husband told me that we should have to make some sort of rough hospital in one of them, as the Residency hospital, where the wounded had been taken, was built of plaster and would not be bullet-proof; so we set to work to get blankets and sheets down from the house, and everything we thought might be useful.

Meanwhile shells were doing dreadful damage over our heads, and we were afraid they might set fire to the thatch and force us out of our temporary shelter. Luckily most of them went over the house into the garden at the back, where they could not do such serious damage; but the noise the guns made, added to the other firing, which had never ceased, was deafening.

There was not the slightest doubt by this time that our position was about as bad as it could very well be. I seemed paralyzed with fear, and it was only by forcing myself to do something, and never thinking or imagining for one moment what the end of it all might be, that I kept my senses sufficiently to be able to make an effort to help the rest. I heard that the wounded were to be brought up to the house immediately, as the hospital was getting too hot for them to remain in it. Poor fellows! they had endured so much as it was in getting there, that it seemed very hard to be obliged to move them again so soon, and take them up to the Residency.

There were a good many of us in the cellar by this time—Mr. Quinton, Colonel Skene, my husband and myself, Mr. Cossins, and Mr. Gurdon.

It was about seven o'clock, and a lovely evening. The sun was just setting, and the red glow of the sky seemed to illuminate the landscape around and the faces of the colonel and my husband as they stood in the doorway talking together in low tones. It was no difficult matter to read what was written on both their faces, and I did not dare ask what was going to happen.

At last my husband came and told me that we were to leave the Residency, and try and find our way to Cachar. It seemed worse to me to think of going out of the house than to remain there; but whatever was to take place had to be at once, and there was no time to spend in giving way to the terrible fear which possessed me. However, a further consultation was held, and it was decided to make a truce with the regent, and put an end to hostilities by coming to some terms with him. A letter was written, which the Chief Commissioner signed. It ran as follows:

"On what condition will you cease firing on us, and give us time to communicate with the Viceroy, and repair the telegraph?"

While this letter was being written, the colonel had ordered our buglers to sound the "cease fire," which they did at once; but it was some time before the Manipuris followed suit. At last their guns ceased, and all was quiet. Then my husband went out with the letter, and called a Manipuri off the wall to take it to the Jubraj. The man went away with it, and my husband returned to the Residency.

Some minutes later a message came to say that the regent wished to see Mr. Quinton and talk over matters with him; and this message was followed by a letter written in Bengali, which contained an acknowledgment of the Chief's letter, and a proposal to the effect that we should surrender our arms if the Manipuris agreed to cease firing. There was some discussion about the translation of part of this letter, and Mr. Quinton proposed that the Jubraj should be called upon to explain the meaning of the passage in question, and asked whether it would be possible to see him.

Meanwhile the Chief Commissioner's party, consisting of himself, Colonel Skene, Mr. Cossins, Lieutenant Simpson, and my husband, had gone down to the office at our entrance gate, and waited there while the regent's letter was being translated. Mr. Simpson had gone of his own accord, as he wished to accompany my husband, and I had begged to be allowed to go with him too; but he said I was safer where I was, and bade me good-bye, telling me to keep a brave heart, that the firing was at an end, and peace about to be restored; and he told me to try and get some rest, as I looked so tired. I never saw him again.

CHAPTER XV.

I REMAINED where he had left me, alone for some minutes, though some of the officers were standing just outside the door of the cellar where I was sitting. It seemed so hard that I could not go with my husband. I feared being left alone without him, and felt very lonely and broken-hearted among so many men, mostly strangers to me. I knew, too, that they would look upon me as an extra burden, and wish me very far away.

I was roused to action by the doctor, who had taken advantage of the truce to get his wounded brought up from the hospital to the house, and had come up first to see what kind of a place could be got ready. I showed him the cellars, for there were several, which all communicated with each other, and formed the entire basement of the house.

Shortly afterwards the Kahars* arrived, carrying poor Mr. Brackenbury on a mattress, and the others followed fast, so that the small cellar was very soon quite full of men lying side by side on the stone floor. The blankets and sheets that we had already collected were very useful, and I made several journeys up to the house, and gathered up every kind of covering from every direction, and all the pillows I could find. A little cooking-stove proved of great service. I fixed it securely upon a table in one corner which I reserved for cooking operations.

The soup we had made on the previous day was in great request. Fortunately there was a large quantity of it, to which I added the contents of five or six tins which I found in the store-room. Milk was the difficulty. All the cows were out in the grounds, and many of them had strayed away altogether and we could not get any milk from them, so were obliged to fall back on condensed milk, of which we also had several tins.

Some of the men were terribly wounded, but

* Kahars—hospital assistants.

poor Mr. Brackenbury was by far the worst. His legs and arms were all broken, and he had several other injuries besides. It seemed a marvel that he was still alive and fully conscious to all that was going on around him. The doctor attended to him first of all, and had bound up his broken limbs, and done as much as possible to alleviate his sufferings; but it was a terrible sight to see the poor lad in such agony, and be so powerless to lessen it in any way. He was very thirsty, and drank a good deal of soup and milk, but we could not get him into a comfortable position. One minute he would lie down, and the next beg to be lifted up; and every now and then his ankle would commence bleeding, and cause him agony to have it bound up afresh. His face was gray and drawn, and damp dews collected on his forehead from the great pain he was suffering.

That scene will never be forgotten—the little cellar with a low roof, and the faces of the wounded lying together on the floor. We did not dare have a bright light for fear of attracting attention to that particular spot, and the doctor did his work with one dim lantern. Such work as it was, too! Every now and then he asked me to go outside for a few moments while the dead were removed to give a little more space for the living.

There were some terrible sights in the cellar that night—I pray I may never see any more like them; but being able to help the doctor was a great blessing to me, as it occupied my attention, and gave me no time to think of all the terrible events of the day, and the wreck of our pretty home. I was very weary, too—in fact, we all were—and when at about half-past ten I asked everybody to come and get some sort of a dinner, they seemed much more inclined to go to sleep, and no one ate much.

The dinner was not inviting, but it was the best that could be got under the circumstances, for I had had to do it all myself. One or two of the servants still remained, but they cowered down in corners of the house, and refused to move out or help me at all. Perhaps had we known that it was our last meal for nearly forty-eight hours, we should have taken care to make the most of it; but no thought of what was coming entered our minds, and long before the melancholy meal was ended most of the officers were dozing, and I felt as though I could sleep for a week without waking.

We all separated after dinner about the house. I went back to the hospital for a little, and found the doctor wanted more milk, so I returned to the dining-room, where I was joined by Captain Boileau, and we sat there for some time mixing the condensed milk with water, and filling bottles with it, which I took downstairs. It was quieter there than it had been. The wounded had all been attended to, and most of them had fallen asleep. Even Mr. Brackenbury was dozing, and seemed a little easier, and only one man was crying out and moaning, and he was mortally wounded in the head. So finding I could do no more there, I went upstairs again, resolving, if possible, to go to my room and lie down for a little while and sleep, for I was very tired.

I went sorrowfully through our once pretty drawing-room, where everything was now in the wildest confusion, and saw all the destruction which had overtaken my most cherished possessions. There are those who imagine that in a case like this a woman's resource would be tears; but I felt I could not weep then. I was overwhelmed at the terrible fate which had come upon us, and too stunned to realize and bewail our misfortunes.

Perhaps the great weariness which overcame me may have helped me to look passively on my surroundings, and I walked through the house as one in a dream, longing only to get to some haven of rest, where I could forget the misery of it all in sleep.

I wended my way to the bedroom through a small office of my husband's, but when I reached the door I found it would not open, and discovered that part of the roof had fallen in, caused by the bursting of a shell. So I gave up the idea of seeking rest there, and retired to the veranda.

I went down the steps and stood outside in the moonlight for a few minutes. It was a lovely night, clear and bright as day! One could scarcely imagine a more peaceful scene. The house had been greatly damaged, but that was not apparent in the moonlight, and the front had escaped the shells which had gone through the roof and burst all round at the back. The roses and heliotrope smelt heavy in the night air, and a cricket or two chirped merrily as usual in the creepers on the walls.

I thought of the night before, and of how my husband and I had walked together up and down in the moonlight, talking of what the day was to bring, and how little he had thought of such a terrible ending; and I remembered that poor lad lying wounded in the cellar below now, who only twenty-four hours ago had been the life and soul of the party, singing comic songs with his banjo, and looking forward eagerly to the chances of fighting that might be his when the morning came.

I wondered where my husband was, and why they had been away so long. They would be hungry and tired, I thought, and might have waited to arrange matters till the next day, as they had apparently been successful in restoring peace. I had an idea of wandering as far as the gate to see whether the party was visible, but on second thoughts I went back into the veranda, and resolved to wait there until my husband should return.

There was one of the officers asleep in a

chair close to me, and I was about to follow his example, when Captain Boileau came out, and I went to him and asked him if he would mind going down to the gate and finding out whether he could hear or see anything of the Chief Commissioner's party, and if he came across any of them to say I wanted my husband. He went off at once, and I fell into a doze in the chair.

It was about twelve o'clock at this time. I do not know how long I had been asleep, when I was awaked suddenly by hearing the deafening boom of the big guns again, and knew then that it was not to be peace.

For a few seconds I could not stir. Terror seemed to have seized hold of me, and my limbs refused to move; but in a minute I recovered, and ran through the house down to the cellar again, where everyone had become alive to the fact that all was over for us. Where was my husband? What had become of them all? This thought nearly drove me mad with anxiety. I could not imagine what their fate had been, but I knew the anguish of mind my husband would endure when the sound of those terrible guns would tell him that we were being attacked again, as he knew we were almost powerless to make any resistance, through lack of ammunition.

We knew that our one chance lay in retreating, as that move had been meditated by Colonel Skene early in the evening, before the truce had taken place; so after an hour had gone by the doctor began moving the wounded out of the cellar, as an immediate retreat had been decided upon.

We were still without any definite tidings of the position of Mr. Quinton and my husband, and the other officers who had accompanied them, and our anxiety on their behalf increased every hour.

It took a long time to get all the wounded on to the grass outside. Mr. Brackenbury was moved first. Poor lad! he begged so hard to be left in peace where he was, and the moving caused him terrible agony. One by one all the poor fellows were helped out, until only a few remained. I gave my arm to one of these, and we were going out through the cellar door, when we were met by four Kahars, carrying someone back into the hospital. The moonlight shone down upon them as they came, and lit up the white face of him they carried, and I saw that it was Mr. Brackenbury. The movement had killed him, and he had died on the grass outside a few seconds after leaving the cellar. Better thus than if he had lived a few hours longer to bear the pain and torture of our terrible march; but it made one's heart ache to leave that young lad lying there dead, alone in the darkened cellar. I went back there just before we left the place, and covered him up gently with a sheet that was lying on the ground, and I almost envied him, wrapped in the calm slumber of death, which had taken all pain and suffering away.

I had no hope that we should ever succeed in making our escape, and it seemed almost useless even to make the attempt. All was ready, however, by this time for our departure, and I went out too, hoping that the Manipuris would soon set fire to the house, which would prevent any indignities being heaped upon the dead by their victorious enemies.

Outside the noise was deafening. Shells burst around us at every turn, and kept striking the trees and knocking off great branches. All idea of going up into the house had to be abandoned, so I could not get a hat or cloak or anything for the journey before us, and had to start as I was. Just before lunch-time I had taken off the close-fitting winter gown which I had put on in the morning, and instead had arrayed myself in a blue serge skirt and white silk blouse, which gave me more freedom for my work in the hospital. I could not have chosen better as far as a walking costume went, and should have been all right if only I had been able to collect a few outdoor garments—hat, cloak, and boots, for instance. As things happened, I was wearing on my feet thin patent leather slippers, which were never meant for out-of-door use, and my stockings were the ordinary flimsy kind that women generally wear. My dress had got soiled already in the hospital, and was not improved by the march afterwards; but I managed to get it washed when we eventually reached British territory, and have it by me to this day. It will be preserved as an interesting relic.

CHAPTER XVI.

THE bustle and confusion outside were great. The Sepoys were being mustered into marching order, but around them on all sides people were rushing about, knocking each other over in their eagerness to make good their escape. These were chiefly servants, Bunnias,* and the many followers who accumulate wherever a regiment goes.

I stood for some time watching them tearing away, until a sudden fear took hold of me that I had been forgotten and left behind. I was meditating going myself, but on second thoughts I remembered I had promised the officers to remain where I was, and they had said they would come for me; and just at that moment one of them came and told me that we were to make a move.

* Bunnias—grain-sellers, provision merchants.

Out in the open, away from the shelter of the house, with one's life in one's hands, as it were, my senses nearly left me. The noise was awful, for besides the bursting of the shells, the firing was heavier than it had been before. I had not gone six yards from the house when a shell exploded almost at my feet, knocking off some branches of a big tree close by, and wounding me very slightly in the arm. I jumped behind the tree, in the vain hope that its broad trunk might save me from further injury, and there I remained for some seconds. The scurrying of those going towards the river awoke me to my senses again, and off I went, too, forgetting to look for my companion, from whom I had managed to get separated.

It was no easy matter to get on to the Cachar road from the back of the Residency, as there were many obstacles in the way. The inner garden was separated from the outer compound by a tall hedge, composed of thorns and sharp twigs. I had superintended the erection of this hedge myself. We had kept a great many cows, and they were always making their way into the flower-garden and destroying the rose-bushes.

Nothing seemed to keep them out until we made this thorn hedge, and that, as I remarked to my husband when I took him to see it first, "was calculated to keep an army of men out if it came to the point."

Fortunately, by the time I arrived at this hedge it had become much broken down, the result of the energy of those who had already gone through it. I found a convenient hole, and got through with comparatively little damage to my raiment; but my hands received a good many scratches, and my poor stockings were dreadfully torn. However, on I went, perfectly insensible as to who were travelling with me. The next obstacle was a mud wall, low enough on our side, but with a six-foot drop on the other. I found myself sitting on the top of this, wondering how I was going to make the descent of the other side, when someone gave me a gentle push, as a sort of warning that I was stopping the traffic, and I slid gracefully down on the other side into the arms of a friendly Bunnia, who also helped me down the river bank, which was very slippery and muddy. I fell two or three times, doing considerable damage to my already dirty dress;

but I got to the water's edge at last, and made a valiant effort to cross the river.

Fortunately for us, it was March, and not April or May; for had these events taken place later in the year, I do not know how we should have crossed that river. But as it was the end of the cold weather, and the rains had not commenced, the stream was low and easily waded. I did not know how deep it was, for we had never crossed it riding, as we generally did Manipuri rivers. We had often thought of doing so, but the banks were so steep and slippery that my husband said it would do the horses no good to clamber down them, and then we might find the river too deep to ford.

So with this delightful uncertainty about things, I made my first plunge, and stepped into the water, which was dreadfully cold. I had got into the middle of the stream, when I was overtaken by the doctor, who seemed rather astonished at finding me there alone. However, I explained to him that I had been too frightened to remain at the house when I saw so many people running away, and had managed fairly well up to that time, but I did not like the river.

He was certainly a good Samaritan on this occasion, for he carried me the rest of the way through the water, and was just about to land me high and dry on the bank, when his foot slipped in the mud, and down we went. We soon picked ourselves up, however, and scrambled out, and then I found that the heel had come off my shoe in the water. I was covered with mud and shivering with cold, for my skirts were dripping with water and very heavy. But there was no time to be lost, and I climbed up the bank and crossed the road, on the other side of which was a deep ditch, into which I retreated and lay down, for firing was going on, and I did not know from which side it came, whether from our men, who had all caught me up by this time, or the Manipuris. Whenever I heard shots afterwards I used to be alarmed, for I never could tell when our men were firing, and always feared the worst, unless I was actually in the midst of the Sepoys, and could see them shooting with my own eyes.

We waited in the ditch some time, until all the Sepoys had crossed the river, and then we started off again to find the way to Cachar. We went some way in the opposite direction at first, and had to come back again; but at length we turned down on to the right road, and commenced the march in real earnest. It was a moonlight night, which enabled us to see quite plainly. Had it been dark, our difficulties would have been increased tenfold. We could not march fast, for the wounded had to be brought along with us, and the number of Kahars carrying them was limited. What they must have endured no one can imagine, being jolted along for so many hours together without any food or rest. I knew every inch of the road we were travelling, as I had ridden down and up it so often in my journeys to and from Cachar, and I was able to give the others the benefit of my knowledge.

We marched along in silence for some miles. At a place called Burri Bazaar we were fired on, but we were not followed from the palace, as we had fully expected. Whether they did not know we had escaped, or whether they thought discretion the better part of valour, and preferred remaining behind the shelter of their stone walls, to following after us with hostile intent, I cannot say. But it was fortunate for us that they gave us the start, and let us get some distance away before they attempted to pursue us.

CHAPTER XVII.

It was about two in the morning that we left the Residency, and we marched steadily on until daybreak. We had not gone four miles away from the station, when I turned to look back, and found the whole sky for miles round lit with a red glow, whilst from among the trees surrounding our house flames were leaping up. Those only who have feelings of affection for the places where they live, and which they call home, can picture what that burning house meant for me.

All we possessed was there—all our wedding presents, and everything that goes towards making a place homelike and comfortable; and these were being destroyed under my very eyes, while I, like Lot's wife of old, had to turn my face in an opposite direction, utterly powerless to avert the terrible destruction which was overtaking all I valued.

I thought of my husband, who I believed to be a prisoner in the palace, surrounded by enemies, witnessing the demolition of the house, and not knowing where I was, or what had become of me. He would see the flames, and hear those terrible guns booming out at every second, and he would know that I was either flying for my life or dead, but no more. And yet I thought he was better off than we were. All hoped that Mr. Quinton and his party would be quite safe, even though they were prisoners, safer than we were; and I myself, knowing the Jubraj so well, thought that he would be clever enough to see his own advantage in keeping them as hostages, even if he were not influenced by feelings of friendship for my husband. And with this reflection I had to quiet my own misgivings. But it was hard to march on in silence without giving way, and it was only by resolving not to look back at all that I managed to restrain my feelings.

I was glad when the dawn came. Every misfortune seems so much harder to bear at night, and there is something in the daylight which gives us strength. If we are ill, we always seem worse during the night; if in sorrow, it is harder to bear in the dark when we are awake and the world is sleeping. And so with myself at this time. The daylight seemed to lessen the horror of the whole situation, and when the pink flush of the dawn came, it mingled with the red glow caused by our burning home, until all was merged into the full light of the rising sun. Then we halted, and had a consultation as to what route we were to pursue. If we went straight on for another six or seven miles, we knew we should have to pass a large Thana strongly garrisoned. On the other hand, if we forsook the main road and took to the hills, we stood the chance of losing our way altogether.

Our great hope was to meet with Captain Cowley and his detachment of two hundred men, who, we knew, were marching up from Cachar. They had commenced their journey to Manipur some days before the rebellion had taken place, and did not know anything of the sort was likely to occur. We knew they were due at a place called Leimatak, some thirty miles from the capital, on the 25th, so that if they had kept to their dates, they could not be more than twenty miles away from us at that moment.

It was the early morning of the 25th when we found ourselves debating over the road, twelve miles away from Manipur. It was decided at length to cut across the fields, and make our way over the hills, hoping to strike the Cachar road again at a higher point, and avoid the Bishenpur Thana.

So we started off again. I was then very exhausted. We had had no food, and the water we met with was very dirty. My feet were cut and sore from the rough walking I had already had, and my clothes still damp and heavy. By this time the sun was fairly high in the heavens, and beat down upon my uncovered head, threatening me with a bad headache at the least, and possibly sunstroke. It was quite evident that some sort of headgear must be provided, so after trying a turban, which I found insufferably hot and heavy, one of the officers gave me his helmet, and wore the pugaree himself. Our way lay for some distance across Dhan-fields.* Owing to the heavy dew which had fallen during the night, these were very wet and soppy, and we were glad when we reached the first hill and began the ascent.

We had been unmolested for some hours now, but the boom of the guns and the crack of the bullets hitting the walls of the house had left such an impression on me that I fancied firing was still going on, and could scarcely believe the others when they told me nothing of the kind was taking place, for the noise in my ears was dreadful.

The first hill was very steep, but only a foretaste of what was to come later on. It was covered with short straggling green grass, interspersed with the rough stubble of last year, which had originally been several feet high, but had been burned, according to the custom in those parts. Here and there a long tough end that had escaped the fire hit one in the face, covering one with smuts, and leaving a black mark where it had touched one, so that after a

* Dhan—rice.

very short time we all looked more or less like sweeps.

The hill we were climbing had a small plateau about three-quarters of the way up, and we steered for this, intending to have a really long halt, and hoping to find water. It was a shady little spot, and when we did reach it, we were all glad to lie down and rest after our terrible exertions. We had a wide view of the plain and the road by which we had travelled, so knew we should be able to note at once if the enemy were pursuing us, and could afford to give ourselves a little breathing space. Water had been found, as we expected, quite near, and as it was much cleaner than what we had discovered in the fields below, everyone drank a good deal, and the Sepoys filled up their bottles with it.

I do not know how long we remained here, as I went to sleep almost at once on our arrival; but when I woke up at last, the others were moving on up the hill, and I had to go too with them. Some distance behind we noted a crowd of natives following us. It was difficult to distinguish whether they were Manipuris or Nagas, but as they were armed with spears and Daôs,* we concluded they must be the latter. Manipuris would have had rifles.

They never came very close to us, for fear of being shot themselves; but we could see them the whole time dancing behind us, shouting and waving spears about. Once or twice they were fully within range, and we could have shot some of them; but it was hardly worth while, and our ammunition was none too plentiful. A terrible fate would have overtaken any straggler who might have fallen behind without the means to defend himself. His head would have been captured as a glorious trophy, carved off while he was alive, for these tribes never trouble about killing their victim first before taking his scalp unless he offers great resistance.

We had reached by this time an elevation of about 4,000 feet above sea-level, and knew that more than 2,000 feet at least still awaited us to be climbed before the top of the ridge could be reached. The Leimatak hill, towards which point we were travelling, was 6,700 feet high, and was

* Daôs—knives.

the topmost peak of the first range of hills lying between us and Cachar.

We clambered on steadily, but very slowly. I was so tired that I could hardly put one foot in front of the other, and felt much more inclined to lie down in the jungle and go to sleep, than to march on. We were very hungry, but I think I suffered less in that respect than the men did; for though I should have eaten probably as heartily as the rest had we possessed food, as there was none to be got, I never thought much about it. Sleep seemed much more desirable.

It was two o'clock on the morning of the 25th that we left the Residency, and it was now between three and four in the afternoon. Every fresh hill seemed worse than its predecessor, and at last we began ascending one which appeared almost impossible to climb. Its sides were very steep and rocky, and there was only the merest apology for a path to direct us in any way. It was a case of using hands and knees to perform the ascent, and it seemed as though we should never reach the summit. When, after wearily toiling on for some hours, we did arrive at the top, I felt that I could not move another step.

We did halt for a short time here, and while we waited an incident occurred which touched me very much. A young Naga, who had been a Sais* in our service for several months at one time, found his way to our camp at the risk of losing his life had he been discovered by the enemy, and presented me with three eggs, expressing at the same time his sorrow at not being able to do more for me. He stayed till sunset with us, and then crept back under cover of the darkness to his village. I was much touched at this simple act of kindness, and I have often remembered it since, and wished it were in my power to do something for the brave lad. But unfortunately I have forgotten his name, and that of the village to which he belonged.

Three eggs are not many among eight hungry people, not to speak of the Sepoys; but no one would share them with me, in spite of my begging them to do so. I could not manage a raw egg, though I made several valiant efforts to swallow

* Sais—groom.

one. Eventually they all came to a bad end, for the two remaining ones were put into somebody's pocket for safety, and were smashed later on, so no one benefited much by the little Naga boy's well-meant offering.

While we were halting on the top of this hill, one of the officers took a few men with him and went on to take stock of the surrounding country, as our exact whereabouts seemed uncertain. He came to a Manipuri Thana before he had proceeded far, and had a parley with the native officer in command there, who called to him, telling him he had something to say. So the party went up to within speaking distance, and the Manipuri called out that he had orders to "pass the Memsahib and Sepoys, but that all the officers must return to Manipur."

However, as soon as he was told that our party intended proceeding undivided, he ordered his men to fire on us, which they immediately did, and we had to begin marching again down the hill and up the other side of the ravine. The firing continued on both sides the whole time, and it was only when we eventually reached the summit of the opposite hill to that upon which we had halted, and disappeared over the crest, that it ceased.

The sun had set, and night was beginning to close in and put an end to the longest day I have ever known. It seemed months almost since our departure from the Residency, and yet it was but twenty-four hours.

How I envied my husband and the others, who, as I then thought, were at any rate in comparative safety, able to eat and sleep, even though they were prisoners! Not that anxiety on my husband's account did not trouble me. I longed to know how he was being treated, and whether they would tell him of my escape, and spare him the torture of not knowing my fate, for I knew how he would fret over it if he did not know.

It seemed so terrible to be obliged to march away leaving them all behind, and at times I longed to hurry back and see for myself what was happening, while, again, I would have given anything to have reached Cachar, and been able to send up help to those in captivity. We thought that Mr. Melville had been made prisoner and brought back to Manipur, as a rumour to that effect had reached us on the 24th, and in that case we supposed he would be with the Chief and his party, a prisoner in the palace.

Perhaps the utter weariness of body and mind which threatened to overcome me at this time prevented my brooding too much on the possible fate of those we had been forced to leave in the hands of their enemies, and it may have been well that it was so.

All that terrible night we tramped on, I with bare feet, as my thin shoes had given out long since. At length, about one o'clock in the morning, we halted in a small grove of trees, lying in a hollow between two hills. We had marched more than twenty miles, and rest was absolutely essential. Here we lay down and slept. The officers gave me their great-coats and bore the intense cold themselves, and I slept as I have seldom slept in a comfortable bed at home, never waking once until someone aroused me about half-past three in the morning, and told me the weary tale again—we were to move on.

The first glimmer of dawn was appearing as we commenced marching again—hungry, tired, and dispirited. No one knew the way, and we only had rough paths here and there to guide us through the jungle; but the actual walking was not so difficult, as we were travelling along the top of a ridge of hills, and had no very steep ascent or descent.

Every now and then we were able to see the Leimatak peak, still some distance off, which I had recognised and pointed out to the others, and I knew that the road to Cachar passed right through a small grove of trees on its summit, so we made it our landmark.

The chances of meeting Captain Cowley's party seemed growing less every hour. Had he been obliged to turn back? we wondered. Would he have gone on towards Manipur, and have passed the place where we hoped to strike the road? We knew nothing.

We were all utterly weary, and dispirited from want of food and rest. It was now the morning of the 26th, and we had none of us tasted food since the 24th. I was so tired that I wished I were dead more than once, and everything seemed quite hopeless, when we came upon the road suddenly.

I think from this moment fate favoured us. We had entertained so little hope of finding the road at all, that it seemed a piece of good fortune when we came upon it suddenly, even though we had all our work still before us and were without food.

The next thing that happened cheered our drooping spirits not a little. We came round a corner and found three Manipuri Sepoys sitting by the roadside, with their arms and accoutrements by them, cooking their morning meal. They were taken by surprise at our sudden advent, and two of them fled, leaving the third a prisoner in our hands. He was not so active as the rest, and the Ghoorkas were too quick for him. They tied him up with straps and anything they could find, and the poor creature evidently thought that his last hour had come. He fell on his knees when he saw me, calling me "Ranee, Ranee," and imploring of me to save him. So I spoke to him as well as I could in

Manipuri, telling him not to be frightened; that we did not intend to hurt him.

Meanwhile, the rice they had cooked came in most acceptably, and perhaps, had a disinterested onlooker been present, he might have been very much amused at the eager way we all rushed at it to devour it. How good it seemed, even though there were scarcely two mouthfuls for each one. What there was was received most gratefully, and I felt very selfish at discovering that, in their thoughtfulness for me, the officers had managed to save a small basketful, which no one would touch, and which they insisted on keeping for me. After the rice was disposed of, we questioned the Manipuri we had captured to find out whether he knew anything of Captain Cowley's movements. He told us that he knew the Sahib had arrived at Leimatak on the 25th, and that he had not yet passed along the road towards Manipur. So we were cheered at the tidings, for we knew now that, with any luck, we must meet with the detachment before very long, and could not be more than eight miles away from Captain Cowley at that moment.

The Manipuri went on to say that there were

a number of the enemy lying in wait for us about half a mile further on, and he advised us to take to the jungle again, offering to show us a path that would lead us into Captain Cowley's camp. The idea of more fighting struck terror into my heart, and had I been in command I should have been foolish enough to take the man's advice; but fortunately the others decided without hesitation to go on, and said they did not believe the prisoner was speaking the truth.

We had scarcely gone half a mile when we came suddenly upon a stockade, and as soon as we appeared round the turn in the road which disclosed it to our view, we were fired on from the hillside above us. I threw myself down for protection against the sloping side of the road, but was not allowed to remain there, as the stockade was about to be rushed, and I had to get over it too, as best I could. Fortunately it had been constructed to prevent Captain Cowley's party from getting past that point in the road, and was in consequence easier for us to clamber over, as we had come from the opposite direction; but I knew that it was useless for me to attempt climbing over it, as my dress would be certain to catch on the sharp ends of the bamboos with which the stockade was constructed, and there I should be suspended, an excellent mark for any stray bullet. So I made a rush to the other side of the road, where I lost my footing and fell, rolling down the Khud. But luckily it was not as steep as it might have been, and I managed to scramble up and get round the stockade, helped very considerably by my former friend the Bunnia, before mentioned, who stretched out his leg from a secure position, and I clambered up by it and lay down completely exhausted and panting from my exertions down the hillside.

Meanwhile firing was going on overhead, which was returned by our men, who killed one or two of the enemy. But the latter were so well screened by the trees around them that it was difficult to get a shot at them at all. I do not know how matters might have ended, but suddenly someone called out that there were more men coming up the hill. No one knew who they were, for they were a long way off, and could only be seen every now and then as they appeared in and out of the trees. Sepoys they were we knew, but were they friends or enemies?

I felt too exhausted to get up and look at them, as all the others were doing, until there was an exclamation from someone that the new arrivals were Ghoorkas. I had felt certain that they would turn out to be Manipuris, who would put an end to us in a very short time. But when opinion became divided as to their identity, the longing for life which we all possess so strongly surged up into my brain, driving me nearly crazy with excitement, and hope, that takes so much killing, rose again within me.

Still we were doubtful. We could see as they came nearer that they wore Kharkee, but the uniform worn by the Jubraj's men was almost identical with that of the Ghoorkas. We sounded our bugle, and it was answered by the advancing party; but then we remembered the Manipuri bugle call was the same as that of the 43rd Ghoorka Rifles, to which regiment Captain Cowley belonged. We got out our only pocket-handkerchief, tied it to a stick, and waved it about, but we could not see whether that signal was returned or not. The time which had elapsed since they were first sighted seemed hours; it was in reality only a few minutes.

Gradually they advanced nearer, running up the hill as fast as they could, and then the majority cried out that they were the Ghoorkas from Cachar. I shut my eyes, for I could not bear the strain of watching them while their identity was uncertain. But at last a Sahib was descried amongst them, and all doubt was over; they were the Ghoorkas, and we were saved. I remember someone asking me if I would make one last effort and run down the hill to meet them, as the firing was still going on, and a stray bullet might even then find its billet; and I remember getting up, with a mist in my eyes and a surging in my head, and running as I have never ran before or since down the hill, helped along by two of the officers.

I remember putting my foot on a stone which rolled away from under it, and gave my ankle a wrench which sprained it, and turned me sick and giddy with pain; and I remember meeting Captain Cowley, and seeing his men rushing past me up the hill, and then I remember nothing more for some time. I did not faint, but I believe I sat down on the side of the road and sobbed, for the strain had been more than I could bear after all the horrors of the previous two days, and tears were a relief.

CHAPTER XVIII.

We were saved! That was the one thought in my mind when I was able to recover my senses sufficiently to be able to think at all. Saved from the terrors of starvation, and from the hands of our enemies; and in my heart I thanked God for having given me the strength which had enabled me to bear all the misery and weariness of the last few days. We human beings are so given to forgetfulness, and fail so often to remember that we owe thanks to Providence for preserving us when man's help is of no avail. We are ready enough to thank our fellow-men for what they do for us, but we forget the rest. This time I can honestly say that I thanked God from the bottom of my heart.

As I sat there by the side of the road, bereft of everything I possessed in the world save only the clothes I wore, I did not think of what I had lost, but only of the life that was still mine. This world is very good and pleasant to live in. Home and friends are very dear to one at all times. But all these are never so precious as when we see them slipping from our grasp, and feel that even our breath, and the life-blood coursing through our veins, are to be taken from us; then alone do we fully rouse ourselves to action, while we struggle and fight for the life that is so dear.

It was some time before I recovered my senses sufficiently to be able to join with the rest in giving the rescuing party a detailed account of our miraculous escape. Some of Captain Cowley's men were still pursuing the now-retreating foe, and we could hear shots being fired from the brow of the hill above us. We remained where we were for some time, and our rescuers produced biscuits and potted meat and soda-water. They had whisky with them too, so we really felt we had fallen on our feet. I was too exhausted to eat much, and did not feel at all hungry; but I was glad enough to drink a peg,*

* Peg—whisky and soda.

and felt very much better for it. My ankle was very painful, so the doctor, who was among the newcomers, bound it up for me, and I went to sleep by the roadside for a short time.

I have said we were saved, but that does not mean that we were entirely out of danger of being fired upon by the Manipuris. They had not spared Captain Cowley's party, though they had allowed him to march up to within twenty miles of us without making themselves unpleasant. But the night before he met us he had marched as usual into a new camping-ground, wholly ignorant of what had occurred in Manipur, and to his great surprise had been fired on. Shortly afterwards fugitives from our party arrived, and told him that we were wandering about in the jungle with every chance of coming to grief before very long, unless rescued. This news was startling, to say the least of it, and caused him to hurry on to our help. When, some miles away, he heard shots being fired from the top of the hill, he concluded that we were not far off, and before long caught sight of the stockade and arrived in the nick of time with men, food, and ammunition to our aid.

The rest of our march was a different thing to what the commencement had been, though discomforts were still many and great. Food was none too plentiful for the Sepoys, though we did not fare badly, and after two days of starvation one is not particular. The 43rd had got a supply of beer, whisky, and cocoa, which were all most acceptable commodities, and I was able to get other luxuries from one of the party, viz., a brush, a sponge, a grand pair of woollen stockings, and some Sepoys' boots, which each measured about a foot and a half in length and were broad in proportion. However, beggars can't be choosers, and as my ankle was very much swollen the commodious boots did not come amiss.

After we had rested some hours we pushed on down the hill to Leimatak, which place was reached before sunset. I was carried in a dooly, as my ankle was too painful to allow of my walking.

When we arrived at the camp we found a string of elephants and mules, which had been travelling up with the detachment, and which had been left behind by Captain Cowley when he discovered the state of affairs we were in, and had to hurry on to our help. It seemed difficult to realize that we were still in a hostile country, surrounded by enemies, for the camp looked just the same as it had done in more peaceful regions.

I had travelled down from Shillong, in the winter of 1890, with the 43rd Ghoorka Rifles, and was consequently quite accustomed to the bustle and movement accompanying a regiment on the march.

We halted at Leimatak for four or five hours, and had a very repectable dinner, to which we did full justice. Afterwards I lay down and went to sleep again, until it was time to move on.

From this time our march was very monotonous. We got up at three every morning and marched until sunset. We had a meal of army rations and cocoa in the morning, and another meal of army rations and beer in the evening, after which we all went to sleep as we were, and never woke until the bugle sounded the reveille.

We were always dead-tired. The hills were very steep, and as we got nearer Cachar the heat was intense during the day, and the cold piercing at night. We could only move very slowly, and with caution, for we never knew when we might be attacked. Pickets were posted all around us on the hills at night, for the purpose of keeping a look-out against the enemy.

We were fired at several times during the march, but the Manipuris did not like the look of a large party, and kept a respectful distance, sometimes firing at us from such a long way off that we did not take the trouble to reply to it. And yet I was more nervous and unstrung at this time than I had been when the danger was really imminent, and bullets coming fast. A stray shot used to make my heart beat with terror, and at last I got so nervous that whenever a shot was fired my companions used to say it was only a bamboo burning in the jungle behind us.

We set fire to nearly all the Thanas on the road, which we found for the most part deserted and empty. At one place called Khowpum, the Manipuris had only left the Thana a few minutes before our arrival. They were lying in wait for us though, on the top of a small ridge, hoping to catch us as we came round the turn of the road. But they were caught themselves, as the Ghoorkas made a small detour and appeared on the top of the ridge instead of below it, and opened fire upon them, causing them to retreat hastily, after a very slight show of resistance.

We then marched into the Thana, and found a quantity of rice in baskets, which had evidently just arrived from the Maharajah's Godowns* for the monthly rations. We could not take the whole amount with us, but the Sepoys were allowed to carry as much as they could, and it was a lucky find. It was often very difficult to procure food for the men, and they had more than once to go without dinner when they got in at night, though as a rule they had half-rations. We had managed to get a supply of rice from one of the Naga villages situated near the road.

The Nagas were for the most part friendly disposed towards us, but here and there they gathered together near their villages, which they had deserted for the meanwhile, and had a stray shot at us as we passed along. We never burned

* Godowns—storehouses.

these villages, thinking they might be useful to the troops when they should return.

I walked most of the way, except the first march after meeting Captain Cowley. He had a pony which he lent me, but the hills were very steep at the best of times for riding, and on this occasion I had to balance myself as best I could on a man's saddle, with the off stirrup crossed over the pony's neck to make some sort of pommel. Riding thus downhill was an impossibility, and I never made the attempt.

My ankle pained me very much at times, but for the most part it seemed to have no feeling in it at all, and was swollen into an unsightly mass.

We came across one or two poor old Manipuri women on the road as we neared the frontier. They had been peaceably travelling up to their homes when the trouble came, and the men with them forsook them to hide in the jungles around until we should have passed by. Poor old ladies! As soon as they saw me they rushed at me and clung to my skirts, refusing to let me out of their sight for a minute. We took them with us to

Cachar and let them remain there until peace should be restored once more.

Day by day brought the same routine: the weary march in the hot sun, and the worn-out slumber at night; but at last the day dawned which was to see us across the frontier in British territory once more, saved in every sense of the word.

It was sunset on the last day of March as we crossed the river Jhiri. I had come all those weary miles through dangers great and terrible, and was alive to tell the tale. Illness had spared us all. We might have had cholera amongst us, to add to the rest of our troubles; but we had been free from that.

To me, a woman, solitary and alone amongst so many men, the march had been doubly trying; but to hear them say that I had not been a burden upon them was some reward for all I had endured.

It has been said lately by some that this retreat to Cachar was in a great measure due to my presence in Manipur at the time, and that my helplessness has been the means of dragging the good name of the army, and the Ghoorka corps in particular, through the mire, by strongly influencing the officers in their decision to effect "the stampede to Cachar."

But I scarcely think that they would have allowed the presence of, and danger to one woman to deter them from whatever they considered their duty; and had they decided to remain at the Residency that night, I should never have questioned their right to do so, even as I raised no argument for or against the retreat to Cachar.

I think that the honour of England is as dear to us women as it is to the men; and though it is not our vocation in life to be soldiers, and to fight for our country, yet, when occasion offers, I have little doubt that the women of England have that in them which would enable them to come out of any dilemma as nobly and honourably as the men, and with just as much disregard for their own lives as the bravest soldier concerned.

But such an insinuation as I have quoted is not, I am happy to think, the unspoken opinion of the many to whom the story of Manipur is familiar. It is but the uncharitable verdict of a few who are perhaps jealous of fair fame honestly won, and who think to take a little sweetness from the praise which England has awarded to a woman.

That such praise has been bestowed is more than sufficient reward for what, after all, many another Englishwoman would have done under similar circumstances.

CHAPTER XIX.

DURING the eventful days which had elapsed between March 23 and April 1, nothing definite had been known by the authorities in India as to Mr. Quinton's proceedings and whereabouts. All that was certain was that he had arrived at Manipur, and had been unable to carry out his original plans for leaving again the day following his arrival, owing to the refusal of the Jubraj to obey the orders of Government; but the tidings of the fight which had followed had never been despatched to head-quarters, owing to the telegraph-wire having been cut immediately after the contest began.

That communication, in this manner, was interrupted was not as serious an omen as might have been supposed. Cutting the telegraph-wire was a favourite amusement of the Manipuris; and even during the small revolution in September,

1890, they had demolished the line in two or three directions.

But when several days went by, and still the wire remained broken, and no information of any kind as to what was going on in Manipur reached the authorities, people became alarmed.

Rumours came down through the natives that there was trouble up there; and a few of the traders found their way into Kohima with the news that all had been killed.

Then excitement rose high, and every day fresh rumours reached the frontier, some of which said that I and one or two others had escaped, but the rest were either killed or prisoners.

The first definite information came from our party. An officer was sent on by double marches on the 31st with the despatches, civil and military; and before another day had passed the whole of India knew the names of those who had escaped, as well as of those who were prisoners, and in a few hours the news had reached England.

To some, that news must have been snatched up with great relief; but there were many who read it with terrible misgivings in their hearts for the fate of those dear to them who were in captivity.

A person who does not know the sensation of never taking his or her clothes off for ten days can scarcely realize what my feelings were when, on arriving at the Jhiri rest-house, I found a bath and a furnished room. Nothing could ever equal the pleasure which I derived from that, my first tub for ten days. I felt as though I should like to remain in it for hours; and even though I had to array myself again afterwards in my travel-stained and ragged garments until I reached Lahkipur, the sensation of feeling clean once more was truly delightful.

I was covered with leech-bites, and found one or two of those creatures on me when I took off my clothes. They had been there three or four days, for we had fallen in with a swarm of them at one of the places where we had camped for the night during the march. It was near a river and very damp, and the leeches came out in crowds and attacked everybody. But the men were able to get rid of them better than I was, and I had to endure their attentions as best I might until we got to the Jhiri, and I could indulge in the luxury of taking off my clothes.

I slept on a bed that night, and was very loath to get up when the bugle awoke us all at the first streak of dawn.

We marched ten miles into a place called Lahkipur, where we found a number of troops already mustering to return to Manipur.

I found clothes and many other necessaries at Lahkipur, which had been sent out for me by the ladies of Cachar; and I blessed them for their thoughtfulness.

The luxury of getting into clean garments was enchanting; and though the clothes did not fit me with that grace and elegance that we womenkind as a rule aspire to, still, they seemed to me more beautiful than any garments I had ever possessed. They were clean; that was the greatest charm in my eyes.

Then came breakfast, such as we had not indulged in for a very long time, and everything seemed delicious.

Immediately after breakfast we all sat down to write home. It was hard work for me after all I had gone through, and with the keen anxiety I was still feeling about those left behind, to put the account of the terrible disaster into words; but I felt that if I did not write then, I should not have the strength to do so later on, and I managed to send a full account home by the next mail.

We halted at Lahkipur all that day, and we started to march our last fourteen miles into Cachar on the night of April 2, or, rather, the early morning of the 3rd. A number of the planters in the neighbourhood came in to Lahkipur to see us before we left, and hear from our own lips the narrative of our escape, and the news of it all got into Cachar long before we ourselves arrived.

Everyone seemed anxious to show us all kindness; but the efforts that were made to secure comforts for me in particular were innumerable as they were generous. When I eventually did arrive at Cachar, I found myself made quite a heroine of. There was not one who did not seem honestly and heartily glad to see me there again safe, and I shall never forget the kindness I received as long as I live.

But amongst them all, there were some old friends who received me into their house, putting themselves out in every possible way to add to my comfort, to whom I owe a debt of gratitude that I never can repay. It would not perhaps be quite agreeable to them if I wrote their names here; but when this record of my terrible adventure reaches them in their far-off Indian home, they will know that I have not missed the opportunity, which is given me in writing about it, of paying them a tribute of gratitude and affection for all their goodness to me in a time of great trouble.

It was delightful to have a woman to talk to again, although my companions on the march had one and all shown me how unselfish and kindhearted Englishmen can be when they are put to the test. They had never let me feel that I was a burden on them, and though often I felt very weak and cowardly, they quieted my misgivings, and praised me for anything I did, so that it gave me courage to go on and help to endure the horrors of that terrible retreat.

For a week I remained with my friends at Cachar, tormented by anxiety concerning my husband. The general opinion seemed to be that he and his companions would be perfectly safe, but I was full of terrible misgivings. I remembered stories of the Mutiny in bygone days, and had read how the prisoners then had often been murdered just at the moment when rescue was at hand.

I feared that when the troops should go back, the Jubraj would refuse to make terms with them, and would threaten to kill the prisoners if our troops came into the place, and I wondered what they would do in that case.

I sent two letters up by Manipuris to my husband, care of the regent, telling him of my escape. I was only allowed to write on condition that I said nothing of the preparations which were being made to rescue Mr. Quinton and his party. But it was a relief to me to be able to write a few lines, for my one idea was to spare my husband the awful anxiety which he would endure until he should hear of my safety.

I had been a week in Cachar when the news came which put an end alike to all hope and all fear. Troops had been hurrying back to Manipur, and the station was alive with Sepoys of all regiments. All the officers and men who had come down with me from Manipur had gone some way on the road back there. The wounded had been placed in the Cachar hospital, where I went to see them two or three times. Poor little fellows! they all seemed so glad to see me.

At last one evening, exactly a week after our arrival, a telegram arrived from Shillong to say that authentic news had come from the regent at Manipur to the effect that all the prisoners had been murdered. I saw the telegram arrive. I was in the deputy commissioner's bungalow when it was handed to him, and made the remark that I disliked bright yellow telegrams, as they always meant bad news.

In India a very urgent message is always enclosed in a brilliant yellow envelope. But the officer said that he did not think anything of them, as he was receiving so many of them at all hours of the day, and for the time I thought no more about it.

Shortly afterwards I noticed that he had left the table. Then I went out too, and met my friend outside, who seemed rather upset about something, and told me she was going home at once. So we went together.

But as soon as we had got into the house she broke to me, as gently and mercifully as she could, the news that my husband had been killed. It was a hard task for her, and the tears stood in her eyes almost before she had summoned up the courage to tell me the worst. And when she had told me I could not understand. The blow was too heavy, and I felt stunned and wholly unable to realize what it all meant. I could not believe, either, that the news was true, for it seemed to me impossible that any authentic intelligence could have been received.

But after a night of misery, made almost heavier to bear by reason of the glimmer of hope which still remained that the news might be false, the morning brought particulars confirming the first message, and giving details which put an end to any uncertainty. The regent had sent a letter saying that the prisoners had been killed. I believe he stated they had fallen in the fight at first, but afterwards contradicted himself, and said they had been murdered by his brother, the Jubraj, without his knowledge or consent.

I cannot dwell on this part of the story. It is all too recent and painful as yet, and too vivid in my recollection. There are no words that can describe a tragedy such as this. Besides, the fate of those captives is no unknown story. All know that through treachery they found themselves suddenly surrounded by their enemies, with all hope of help gone, and without the means to defend themselves.

And the ending—how they were led out one by one in the moonlight to suffer execution, after having been obliged to endure the indignity of being fettered! How, of that small band, one had already fallen dead, speared by a man in the crowd; and one was so badly wounded that he had fallen, too, by the side of his dead friend, and had to be supported by his enemies when he went out, as the others had to go, to meet his fate.

And yet in all that terrible story there is one ray of comfort for me in the fact that my husband was spared the fate of the rest. I am glad to think that he did not suffer. He never heard those terrible guns booming out, proclaiming the work of destruction which was being wrought on the home he had loved. He did not see the cruel flames which reduced our pretty house to a heap of smoking ruins, and he did not know that I was flying for my life, enduring privations of every kind, lonely, wretched, and weary at the outset.

He was spared all this, and I am thankful that it was so. For before the guns commenced shelling us again on that dreadful night, the tragedy described had already taken place within the palace enclosure.

Well for me was it that I was ignorant of my husband's fate. Had I known, when we left the Residency that night, that he and I were never to meet again on God's earth, I could never have faced that march. It had been hard enough as it was to go and leave him behind me; but thinking that he was safe helped me in the endeavour to preserve my own life for his sake.

It is time to end this narrative of my own experiences, for all was changed for me from the day that brought the terrible news; but the account of the incidents of March, 1891, would scarcely be complete without my touching on some other events which were occurring in a different quarter in connection with the Manipur rebellion.

I allude to the noble part taken by Mr. Grant (whom I have referred to earlier in this volume) in the affair as soon as tidings of the disturbance reached him. To describe his share in my own words would scarcely be a satisfactory proceeding, so I have thought it better to add his letter, giving all the details of what occurred, to my own narrative.

The news first reached him on the morning of March 27, and in his letters home he describes the subsequent events as follows:

MAJOR GRANT'S NARRATIVE.

"On March 27, morning, thirty-five men of 43rd Ghoorka Light Infantry came into Tummu, reporting there had been a great fight at Manipur on 25th. Chief Commissioner Grimwood, the Resident, same who came to see me with wife, Colonel Skene, and many others, killed, and five hundred Ghoorkas killed, prisoners, or fled to Assam; the thirty-five men of 43rd Light Infantry had been left at the station Langthabal, four miles south of Manipur, and after the others broke they retreated to Tummu in forty-eight hours, only halting four hours or so, fighting all the way and losing several killed. I wired all over Burmah, and asked for leave to go up and help Mrs. Grimwood and rest to escape, and got orders at eleven p.m. on 27th.

"At five a.m., 28th, I started with fifty of my men, one hundred and sixty rounds each, thirty Ghoorkas, Martini rifles, sixty rounds, and three elephants; marched till five p.m., then slept till one a.m., 29th, marched till two p.m., slept till eleven p.m., marched and fought all the way till we reached Palel at seven a.m., 30th, having driven one hundred and fifty men out of a hill entrenchment and two hundred out of Palel, at the foot of the hills, without loss. Elephants could only go one mile or so an hour over these hills, 6,000 feet high, between this and Tummu, but road very good. Prisoners taken at Palel said that all the Sahibs killed or escaped; Mrs. Grimwood escaped to Assam. Poor Melville, who had stayed a week before with me at Tummu (telegraph superintendent), killed on march.

"I marched at eleven p.m., 30th, and neared Thobal at seven a.m., meeting slight resistance till within 300 yards of river, three feet to six feet deep, and fifty yards broad; there seeing a burning bridge, I galloped up on poor 'Clinker' (the old steeplechasing Burman tal I had just bought on selling my Australian mare 'Lady Alice'), and was greeted by a hot fire from mud-walled compounds on left of bridge and trenches on the right in open all across the river. I saw the wooden bridge was burnt through, and made record-time back to my men, emptying my revolver into the enemy behind the walls.

"My men were in fighting formation. Ten

my men 2nd Burmah Battalion of Punjaub Infantry (new name), and ten Ghoorkas in firing line at six paces interval between each man, and twenty my men in support 100 yards rear of flanks in single rank, and twenty my men and twenty Ghoorkas reserve, baggage guard 300 yards in rear with elephants, and thirty followers of the Ghoorkas (Khasias, from Shillong Hills). We opened volleys by sections (ten men) and then advanced, one section firing a volley while the other rushed forward thirty paces, threw themselves down on ground, and fired a volley, on which the other section did likewise. Thus we reached 100 yards from the enemy, where we lay for about five minutes, firing at the only thing we could see, puffs of smoke from the enemy's loop-holes, and covered with the dust of their bullets. I had seen one man clean killed at my side, and had felt a sharp flick under arm, and began to think we were in for about as much as we could manage; but the men were behaving splendidly, firing carefully and well directed. I signalled the supports to come up wide on each flank; they came with a splendid rush and never stopped on joining the firing line, but went clean on to the bank of the river, within sixty yards of the enemy, lying down and firing at their heads, which could now be seen as they raised them to fire; then the former firing line jumped up and we rushed into the water. I was first in, but not first out, as I got in up to my neck and had to be helped out and got across nearer to the bridge, the men fixing bayonets in the water.

"The enemy now gave way and ran away all along, but we bayoneted eight in the trenches on the right, found six shot through the head behind the compound wall. At the second line of walls they tried to rally, but our men on the right soon changed their minds, and on they went and never stopped till they got behind the hills on the top of the map; our advance and their retreat was just as if you rolled one ruler after another up the page on which the map is.

"When I got to (A) I halted in sheer amazement; the enemy's line was over a mile long. I estimated them at eight hundred, the subadar at one thousand two hundred; afterwards heard they were eight hundred men besides officers.

They were dressed mostly in white jackets with white turbans and dhoties, armed with Tower-muskets, Enfield and Snider rifles, and about two hundred in red jackets and white turbans, armed with Martinis, a rifle that will shoot over twice as far as our Sniders. I simply dared not pursue beyond (A), as my baggage was behind; and beyond them I had seen two or three hundred soldiers half a mile away on my right rear.

"At eight a.m. I was in the three lines of compounds, each compound containing a good house about thirty by twenty feet (one room), and three or five sheds and a paddy-house. We carried over our baggage on our heads, leaving a strong party at (A), and set to work to prepare our position for defence. I had used eighty of our one hundred and sixty rounds per man; only one man was killed. I found I was slightly grazed, no damage, and three of my six days' rations; and I could not hope to reach Manipur, therefore I must sit tight till reinforced from Burmah, or joined by any of the defeated Ghoorka Light Infantry troops from Cachar.

"We filled the paddy-house with paddy, about

a ton, and collected much goor (sugar-cane juice) and a little rice and green dhal and peas from the adjoining houses. Then I cleared my field of fire—*i.e.*, by cutting down the hedges near and burning the surrounding houses and grass; my walls were from two feet to four feet high, and one to three feet thick, and, I thought, enough. Put men on half ata and dhal; shot a mallard (wild duck on river), and spent a quiet night with strong pickets.

"On April 1, at six a.m., my patrols reported enemy advancing in full force from their new position. I went to (A), where picket was, and took a single shot with a Ghoorka's Martini into a group of ten or twelve at 700 yards. The group bolted behind the walls at (B), and the little Ghoorkas screamed with delight at a white heap left on the road, which got up and fell down again once or twice, none of the others venturing out to help the poor wretch.

"Then a group assembled on the hill, 1,000 or 1,100 yards off, and the Ghoorka Jemadar fired, and one went rolling down the hill; I fired again, but no visible effect. The enemy then retired under cover; but at three p.m. they advanced in full force. I lined wall (A) with fifty men; holding rest in reserve in the fort.

"The enemy advanced to 600 yards, when we opened volleys, and after firing at us wildly for half an hour, they again retired to 800 yards, and suddenly from the hill a great 'boom,' a scream through the air; then, fifty feet over our heads, a large white cloud of smoke, a loud report, and fragments of a 9-lb. or 10-lb. elongated common shell from a rifle cannon fell between us and our fort; a second followed from another gun, and burst on our right; then another struck the ground and burst on impact to our front, firing a patch of grass; they went on with shrapnel.

"I confess I was in a horrid funk, for although I knew that artillery has little or no effect on extended troops behind a little cover, I dreaded the moral effect on my recruits, who must have had an enormously exaggerated idea of the powers of guns; but they behaved splendidly, and soon I had the exact range of the guns, by the smoke and report trick, 900 or 970 yards; and after half an hour, during which their fire got wilder and wilder, both guns disappeared, and only one turned up on the further hill, 1,500 yards from (A), from which they made poor practice, as the Ghoorkas' bullets still reached them, and they only ran the gun up to fire, and feared to lay it carefully. All this time the enemy kept up their rifle fire, from 600 to 800 yards, but I only replied to it when they tried to advance nearer.

"By this time it grew dark, and when we could no longer see the enemy we concentrated in the fort, as the enemy had been seen working round to our left. I sent the men back one by one along the hedges, telling each man when and where to go; none of them doubled.

"It was quite dark when I got back, and posted them round our walls, which seemed so strong in the morning, but were like paper against well-laid field-guns; I felt very, very bitter.

"I was proud of the result of my personal musketry-training of my butchas (children), all eight months' recruits, except ten or fifteen old soldiers, who set a splendid example, and talked of what skunks the Manipuris were, compared to the men they had fought in Afghanistan and the North-West Frontier; but they all said they had never seen such odds against them before. Our total day's loss—a pony killed, and one man slightly wounded.

"All night the enemy kept up a long-range fire without result, which was not replied to. I tied white rags round our foresights for night-firing. I slept for about two hours in my east corner, and at three a.m. turned out to strengthen the walls in four places against shell-fire, made a covered way to the water, and dug places for cover for followers. Luckily much of the compound was fresh ploughed, so we only had to fill the huge rice-baskets with the clods, and the ration-sacks, pails, my pillow-case, and a post-bag I had recovered, everything with earth, and soon I had five parapets in front and flanks, each giving cover for eight or ten men. The enemy had retired behind the hill.

"At three p.m. a patrol reported a man flag-signalling. I went out with white flag, and met a Ghoorka of 44th, a prisoner in Manipuris' hands, who brought a letter signed by six or eight Babu prisoners, clerks, writers, post and telegraph men, saying there were fifty Ghoorka prisoners and fifty-eight civil prisoners, and imploring me to retire. If I advanced they would kill the prisoners; if I retired the durbar would release them, and send them to Cachar. I said those prisoners who wished could go to Cachar, and I would retire to Tummu with those who wished to come with me.

"I also wrote to the Maharajah, and also on 2nd, 3rd, 4th, and 5th messages passed from me to Maharajah and his two brothers, Jubraj and Senaputti, the heir and the commander-in-chief.

"Maharajah wrote saying he was not responsible for the outbreak; and Senaputti told the messengers he had 3,000 men in front of me, and would cut us all up.

"I wrote refusing to move without the Ghoorka prisoners at least, and said 'I didn't care for 5,000 Manipuri Babus.'*

"At last Jubraj said the prisoners had been

* Babu—office-clerk; used here as a term of contempt.

sent away to Assam, and sent me 500 pounds ata and 50 pounds each dhal and ghee to retire with. I sent back the rations, and refused to move without a member of the durbar as a hostage, to remain at Tummu till prisoners arrived at Cachar and Kohima. They offered me a subadar. I said he was no one. I had signed all my letters as Col. A. Howlett, Com. 2nd B. Regt., to impress them with my strength and importance, and put on the subadar's badges of rank in addition to my own.

"The next morning (6th) they attacked again at dawn, and as I had only seventy rounds per man for Sniders and thirty for Martinis, I closed into the fort. At first, after forty minutes' shelling, they made determined efforts to cross the walls 100 to 200 yards in front of my front and left; but nearly every man was hit as he mounted the wall, and then they remained firing from behind the walls.

"At eight a.m. a good lot had collected behind the wall 200 yards from my left. I crept out with ten or twelve Ghoorkas, who held my rear and right under the hedge, and drove them with loss by an attack on their right flank, and we bolted back to fort without loss.

"Then at eleven a.m. there was firing from behind the hedges to our front with a weapon that rang out louder than their rifles. I crept out with a havildar and six Ghoorkas close in the ditch under the hedge, out to our front from our right, up to within ten yards of the nearest of them. They opened a wild fire, and bolted as we attacked their left flank; but then we found ourselves in a bit of a hole, for thirty or forty were in a corner behind a wall, six feet high, over which they were firing at us. I had my D. B. sixteen-bore shot-gun, and six buckshot and six ball cartridges, and as they showed their heads over the wall they got buckshot in their faces at twenty yards.

"When my twelve rounds were fired, and the Ghoorkas also doing considerable damage, we rushed the wall, and I dropped one through the head with my revolver, and hit some more as they bolted.

"When we cleared them out we returned to the fort along the ditch, having had the hottest three minutes on record, and only got the

Ghoorka havildar shot through the hand and some of our clothes shot through; we had killed at least ten.

"Next day I visited the corner, and found blood, thirty Snider and fifteen Martini cartridges, and one four-inch long Express cartridge, ·500, which accounted for the unaccountable sounds I had heard.

"Next day I heard I had killed the 'Bhudda' (old) Senaputti, or the commander-in-chief of the old Maharaj, father of the present lot of scoundrels, and also two generals; but that is not yet confirmed.

"Well, as I said, we bolted back into the fort, and I had thirty minutes' leisure to go all round my fort, and found I had only fifty rounds per man, enough for one hour's hard fighting, and only twenty-five for Martinis; so I ordered all the men to lie down behind the walls, and one man in six kept half an hour's watch on their movements. The men had orders not to fire a shot till the enemy were half-way across the open adjoining compounds; but the enemy declined to cross the open, and the men did not fire a shot all day. I picked off a few who showed their heads from the east corner, where I spent the rest of the day, the men smoking and chatting, and at last took no notice of the bullets cutting the trees a foot or six inches over their heads.

"Thus the day passed, the enemy retiring at dark, and we counted our loss—two men and one follower wounded, one by shell; one pony killed, two wounded; two elephants wounded, one severely; and my breakfast spoilt by a shell, which did not frighten my boy, who brought me the head of the shrapnel which did the mischief—I will send it home to be made into an inkpot, with inscription—and half my house knocked down.

"Next day, 7th, quiet, improved post and pounded dhan to make rice.

"Saturday, 8th, ditto. Large bodies of Manipuris seen moving to my right rear long way off.

"At five, 7th, two Burmans came with letters from Maharajah to Viceroy, and a letter from 'civil' to poor killed chief commissioner. I opened and found that large army comes up from Burmah 'at once.' A small party three or four days before would have been more use. Maharajah's letter a tissue of miserable lies and stupid excuses.

"At noon, 8th, white flag appeared, and a man stuck a letter on road and went back. Went and found it contained a letter from Presgrave, with orders from Burmah for me to retire on first opportunity, and he was not to reinforce me, but to help me to retire. I *was* sick, but the orders were most peremptorily worded. So at 7.30 p.m., on a pitch-dark, rainy night, we started back—a splendid night for a retreat, but such a ghastly, awful job!

"We had two wounded elephants with us, and made just a mile an hour, only seeing our hands before our faces by the lightning-flashes. I had to hold on to a Sepoy's coat, as I could see absolutely nothing; but they see better in the dark than we do. We were drenched to the skin, and were halting, taking ten paces forward when the lightning flashed, and then halting the column half an hour at times; but the feeble Manipuri, of course, would not be out such a night, and we passed through three or four villages full of troops without a man showing.

"At two a.m., 9th, a man said sleepily, 'The party has come'—that was all—and the next moment Presgrave had my hand. He had heard that I was captured, and all my men killed or taken at two different places; had returned nearly to Tummu, but the two Burmans with Maharajah's letter told him where I was, and he marched thirty-six hours without kit or rations, only halting for eight hours, and was coming on to Tummu. He went back to meet some rations, and then, after passing the night in a Naga village, returned to Palel and here, with a hundred and eighty men and eleven boxes of ammunition—forty of them our mounted infantry.

"At Palel we found three or four hundred Manipuri soldiers who did not expect us; they saw us half a mile off, and bolted after firing a few shots. I went on with the mounted infantry, and after trotting till within 300 yards of the retreating army, we formed line on the open and went in.

"I rode for a palki and umbrella I saw, and shooting one or two on my way got close up; but a hundred or so had made for the hills on our right and made a short stand, and suddenly down went poor Clinker on his head, hurling me off. Jumped up—I was covered with blood from a bullet-wound in the poor beast's foreleg, just below the shoulder. Two men came up. I twisted my handkerchief round with a cleaning-rod above the wound, stopping the blood from the severed main artery, and, refilling my revolver, ran on.

"By this time the men had jumped off and were fighting with the enemy on the hill; the palki was down, and I fear the inmate of it escaped. We killed forty of them without loss, excepting poor Clinker and another pony. After pursuing three miles we stopped, and returned to the infantry, which were rather out of it, though they doubled two miles. Found poor Clinker's large bone broken, and had to shoot him at once.

"We collected the spoil and returned to camp, where we had a quiet night, and were joined by the Hon. Major Charles Leslie and four hundred of his 2nd-4th* Ghoorkas, and two

* 2nd-4th—2nd Battalion 4th Ghoorkas.